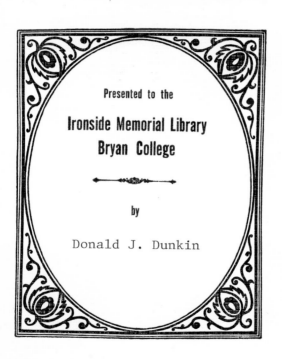

QUIET TALKS ABOUT
THE TEMPTER

QUIET TALKS
ABOUT
THE TEMPTER

BY

S. D. GORDON

Author of "Quiet Talks on Power,"
"Quiet Talks on Prayer"

NEW YORK   CHICAGO   TORONTO
FLEMING H. REVELL COMPANY
LONDON AND EDINBURGH

QUIET TALKS

FIRST SERIES

QUIET TALKS ON POWER

QUIET TALKS ON PRAYER

QUIET TALKS ON SERVICE

SECOND SERIES

QUIET TALKS ABOUT JESUS

QUIET TALKS ON PERSONAL PROBLEMS

QUIET TALKS WITH WORLD WINNERS

THIRD SERIES

QUIET TALKS ON HOME IDEALS

QUIET TALKS ABOUT THE TEMPTER

New York: 158 Fifth Avenue
Chicago: 80 Wabash Avenue
Toronto: 25 Richmond St., W.
London: 21 Paternoster Square
Edinburgh: 100 Princes Street

CONTENTS

INTRODUCTION

These Quiet Talks about the Tempter are really talks about the Spirit-filled life. They necessarily put much emphasis upon our Lord Jesus the *Victor;* upon *Calvary,* the place of Victory; upon *Obedience,* the pathway of Victory; upon *Bible-study* and *Prayer,* the preparation for Victory; and upon *Courage*—faith fighting—the spirit of Victory.

These are homely talks. They have the directness and blunt simplicity, and repetition for emphasis' sake, that mark conversational speech. They were spoken to crowds of men and women, in the thick of the fight, looking for a bit of help. They are put down here in black and white, in response to many requests, practically as they were spoken, and for the same purpose—that some may be helped to better fighting, and to swifter, surer victory.

They are not meant for the scholarly, nor for the argumentative critic, save as these may care to enroll themselves as men looking for any bit of homely help on the road of life. If, by the Master's grace, they help some, who feel the stress of the struggle, to fight better, to sing cheerier, to follow our blessed Master closer; if they may help a little toward purer lives, warmer sympathy, more loving service, keener watching and better praying, their purpose will be served, and the singing of our wondrous Lord Jesus' praise be a bit louder and sweeter.

I.—TEMPTATION

TEMPTATION

Using God's Roads.

Every one is tempted. If a man is alive he
is tempted. If he is living on this particular
planet, called the earth, he is a tempted man.
If he have a body to live in, he will be tempted
through it. If there be a mind to think with,
there is temptation through that. If there be a
social nature to enjoy others through, if there
be a right ambition to take one's place in life,
and do his full share of the fighting, and—in a
good way—win his share of the victory, there
will be temptation because of these.

For temptation always follows the natural
grooves of the true life. Satan always travels
God's road. He never makes any of his own.
He uses God's. There is nothing wrong in
itself. But anything and everything may become damnably wrong. The sin is in the wrong
motive underneath, or the wrong relationship
round about an action. It is in the excess or
the exaggeration.

Speech is a gift from God. But the desire
to deceive through speech—the using of the
power of speech to say what is not true—is
from the evil one. The act of reaching a hand

into a drawer to take out some money may be either right or wrong. Everything depends on whose hand it is, and why it is reaching in. Either one of the very opposite extremes of right or wrong may be in the act.

If that drawer is mine and the money mine, and I am taking it out prayerfully to send the Gospel of Christ to Madagascar, the act is not merely right, but it is specially to be praised. For they need the Gospel in Madagascar, and the money may be transmuted into a redeemed life under the Holy Spirit's touch.

If the drawer is not mine, nor the money it contains, then the act is against the law of man, as well as the law of God. It is a crime as well as a sin.

If the drawer is mine, and the money too, so far as man's reckoning goes, and yet I am taking the money out to use for something that is in no sense a necessity, but only a luxurious indulgence, it becomes a sin, though not a crime. It is a sin of selfishness. And there is no greater sin, nor commoner. It is a misappropriation to my own use of funds entrusted to me by God to be used for Him in making His Gospel known among men. For that is the one purpose that should govern all our possessions. It is a distinct breach of trust.

So it is regarding every action of life. The motive or relationship makes it good or bad.

The same act may be saintly, or, selfishly hellish.

Satan boldly and thievishly appropriates everything for his own uses and purposes. His long fingers reach in everywhere. Nothing is sacred to his touch. The holiest functions, the purest relationships, the most innocent pastimes are subtly and boldly turned by him away from their true uses to serve his own purposes.

Because we are here and sin is here, and things are as they are, we are tempted, and we will be tempted to the last rod of the road. The evil one attends to that. With great craftiness and persistence he sees that the temptations come under some guise or covering.

How to meet Temptation.

Some people *yield* to their temptations, I am sorry to say. They calmly lie down, and are trodden underfoot, like—shall I say like a dog? Of course I mean a dead dog. No live dog would. But some men do.

Some men *play* with their temptations. Their consciences are not dead yet, though they are a bit withered up from lack of exercise. They make a pretence of fighting, and then having thrown that bone to their consciences to be chewed on a bit, they likewise lie down and are trodden underfoot, like their brothers and sisters just referred to.

Some persons _fight_ their temptations. They recognize and resist them. They have learned the meaning of "watch and pray." The "watch" brings into play the human side, the "pray" the divine side. Their watch-tower is never deserted. They have found out the sleeplessness of the tempter, and of all his sub-tempters. They lock up the joints of their will, and limber up the joints of their knees, and they fight. They say, "even though we go down, we will go down fighting, and only in the last ditch, and with face outward toward the foe. And when the sword blade snaps we will use the scabbard. But we will never yield by so much as a half hair's breadth." That's the spirit in which they meet and fight their temptations.

In a certain large steel work a big muscular Scotchman called "Striker Jones" held the position of boss-striker. Nearly all the men in his department were hard drinkers. And he was not an exception to the rule. But a change took place. He became a Christian; and when pressed by his fellows to take a drink he refused. "I shall never take a drink ony mair, lads," he quietly said, "na drunkard shall inherit the Kingdom of God." And they said, "Wait a bit, till the hot weather comes—till July. When he gets as dry as a gravel-pit he will give in. He can't help it." But right through the hottest months he toiled on, the sweat pouring in streams, yet he never seemed to be tempted to drink.

At last the time-keeper of the mill spoke to him as he was giving in his time. He said, "You used to drink a good bit. Don't you miss it?"

"Yes," he said, very emphatically.

"How do you manage to keep away from it?"

"Weel, just this way. It is now ten o'clock, isn't it?"

"Yes."

"Weel, to-day is the twentieth of the month. From seven till eight I asked that the Lord would help. He did. And I put a dot down on the calendar right near the twenty. From eight till nine. He kept me, and I put down another dot. From nine to ten He has kept me, and now I gie Him the glory as I put down the third dot. Just as I mark these dots I pray—'O Lord, help me; help me to fight it off for another hour.'"

That's the fighting spirit for temptations. And it makes no matter what the temptation is, it can be fought and resisted successfully only by steady stiff fighting.

Temptation's Weak Spot.

Now I wish you would mark very keenly this: temptation has no power of itself. It must have help from the man being tempted. There is nothing so weak, so ridiculously weak in itself, as a temptation. It can do nothing, absolutely nothing, without the consent of the man being tempted. It can allure, it can sing bewitching songs, it can make an atmosphere around you mighty hard to breathe in, but it can't get inside a man's life without his consent. And it is as powerless as an infant except as it can get inside.

There is only one knob to the door of a man's life. And that is on the inside. That door never opens except as the man inside opens it. With greatest reverence be it said that God won't come in without a man's glad consent. God never forces. He comes in only by our free consent. And—mark keenly—Satan can't get in without the man's willing consent. Let every tempted man underscore this fact, that it may stand out sharp and clear. And then he can underscore it sharper yet in the book of his experience that it takes two to make a successful temptation, and you are one of the two. Without your partnership the temptation must slink dejectedly away defeated.

A young fellow of seventeen was telling an older friend of an experience he had. He was a carpenter's apprentice, and had been sent to make certain measurements for a new counter in a drinking saloon. It was very cold weather, and his teeth were chattering as he arrived, for his coat was thin. The saloon-keeper immediately mixed a hot drink, and pushed it over the counter to him. "It'll cost you nothing," he said, "drink it down and you'll soon stop shivering, my boy."

"He meant it kindly, too, and didn't think any harm," said the fellow, as he told the story. "That's what made it hard to push it back, and say I didn't want it."

"It must have been a big temptation," said the friend. "That saloon-keeper might have started you on the road to ruin."

"Well," said the young fellow, frankly, "I'd rather have had it than some other kinds. You see *it takes two* to make a successful temptation. There's no saloon-keeper and no cold weather that can make me drink. The temptation I'm most afraid of is the one I'm ready for when it comes, by hankering after it. If I had taken that drink, I would not have put all the blame on that saloon-keeper. It takes two every time to make a successful temptation."

Temptation of itself is utterly powerless. If a man yield, of course, he is whipped in the start; he gives the chance of victory away without even a decent show of fight. If a man play with his temptation, as so many do; if he dally and linger; if he hang round the fire poking dry straws in, as so many do, then he is whipped too.

His defeat is sure. He passes the chance of victory out to the assailant without a decent show of fight.

If a man fight, if he is determined to fight, *he will win.* For such a man will reach out for every bit of help within reach. And there is One standing very near by who knows all about temptation, temptations of every sort, who has been tempted Himself, and who eagerly gives His help. He is always waiting to help.

A man may feel weak and the temptation may seem very subtle and very strong. It may come with the rush of a wild storm down the valley. Or it may come with the sly, sneaking subtlety of a snake crawling along in the tall grass to strike its fangs in when you least think it is there. But the man says, " I mean to be right. I mean to be good, strongly good. I mean to be pure, above all else to be pure." And so he locks up every joint of his will, and reaches eagerly out for the help of the Helper at hand, and he fights, and more—he wins. Every temptation so approached and attacked is already defeated.

How to Win.

Will you mark as keenly as you ever marked anything that there must be two factors on the winning side in that fight? There must be a

determined will, _and_ there must be alongside
the Man who was tempted in all points just as
we are, and who never failed, and who never
fails. Let it be said very plainly that neither
one is enough without the other.

There must be a jaw-locked determination not
to yield. With greatest reverence, be it said,
the Lord Jesus alone without our wills is not
enough. He works _through_ the man's will.
He works with us. He _can_ work only through
us. He strengthens the will. That will may be
very weak. It may be shattered and smashed by
indulgence in sin out of all resemblance to a
will. But, remember, it is never lost. While
there's life, there's a choosing power. However
weak it may be it still can choose. And our
tempted, victorious Lord Jesus will help it to
act, and to act right, no matter how hard it
seems. And then He helps it through that act
of choice.

He will put new life and strength into one
the very moment the determination is decided
upon. And so, bit by bit, sometimes in a way
that seems slow, but very very surely, the new
strength comes into the will. And so through
the choice to resist the wrong and do the right,
our victorious Fellow-Man breathes new strength
in, and gives us the enormous advantage of His
victory and of His presence.

But let it be said, just as bluntly and plainly

as it can be said, that the will alone is not enough. A man may have a square jaw, a hard fist, a head high at the crown, and in other ways give evidences of a ruggedly strong will. But as surely as he goes alone, he will go down, and he will go down sprawling, and he will carry the scars of his fall clear to the end of the chapter of life.

He may not go down for quite a while, and that itself will greatly increase his confidence in himself, but the fall will come to the man going alone. Going alone means going down before you get through. And the longer the fall-down is deferred, the sharper and harder the fall will be when it does come.

There must be a *will,* and there must be more —a Saviour too, a Friend, a Helper. Neither one nor the other, but one *and* the other; a will and a Saviour; a will strengthened and helped by a Saviour; a Saviour tempted in all points, therefore sympathetic; victorious at every point, and therefore strong to help—a Saviour like that working through our wills.

If this wondrous Victor of the Wilderness, and of Calvary, be not allowed to help, there will be a French Waterloo in your life. And the French never talk about their Waterloo. They are a bit busy if that topic is suggested. There is no Waterloo on the famous Napoleon Monument in Paris. The sculptor had a con-

venient lapse of memory just then.   The greatest battle was omitted.

If you will allow this great human Saviour,
who was divine too, to come alongside and help,
there will be an English Waterloo in your life.
Every temptation is a chance for a Victory.
It is a signal to fly the flag of our Victor.   It
is a chance to make the tempter know anew that
he is defeated.   It is an opportunity to strike
the note for a ringing song of victory.   Steady,
steady—there's a will within, and a Friend
alongside, and a victory just ahead, with the
flag high, and the music joyous.

> " Hold on, my heart, in thy believing!
>   The steadfast only wear the crown ;
> He who, when stormy waves are heaving,
>   Parts with his anchor, shall go down ;
> But he whom Jesus holds through all
> Shall stand, though earth and heaven fall.
>
> " Hold out !   There comes an end to sorrow ;
>   Hope from the dust shall conquering rise ;
> The storm foretells a sunnier morrow ;
>   The cross points on to Paradise.
> The Father reigneth, cease all doubt ;
> Hold on, my heart, hold on, hold out." [1]

[1] Schmolke.

II.—THE TEMPTER

THE STORY OF HIS CAREER

The Keynote.

Wherever there is temptation there is a tempter. It tells of him. Whenever it comes, if you will look about a bit, you are sure to find him.

Temptation may come through an evil heart inside. It often does. But there's always something outside, too. And that something is pretty sure to conceal some one. It may come through inner passions or desires. It is very apt to come through a coming together of an inner desire and an outer circumstance.

But however it comes, through the inner, through the outer, or through these two getting together, it always comes from the tempter. The inside longing and the outside opening are simply coverings to hide his approach. He uses whatever is handiest and most usable.

The very name "tempter" tells at once his most striking characteristic. The word itself means that there is something wrong near by. There's somebody being urged to do the thing that is wrong. There's some one, more or less out of sight, doing the urging. The wrong it-

self tells of a right. There is only one right.
Any turning aside is wrong. The only right
thing to do is that right.

And—remember—there is some One else
present, too. The wrong tells of the right, and
the right tells of this other One who is close
by, earnestly longing to have us do the right,
and eager to help us do it. That is the some
One who gave His image to us, and will stop
at nothing to help us in our fight against the
bad.

I want just now to talk with you a bit about
the tempter who is sneaking behind the temptation. It is very striking that the true keynote to
a talk about the tempter is in the name of the
One who is the very opposite of that tempter.
The name of Jesus is the keynote that must give
the pitch to the music here as everywhere else.
For that name " Jesus " means " Victor," lit-
erally " Jehovah-Victor." It is a word taken
bodily over from the old language of the Hebrews into the Greek or Aramaic of our Lord's
time; and thence it has gone into every language where it is found to-day. There is the
shout of victory in the very name.

And, of course, " victor " means that there
has been a victory. And victory tells of a
battle, a fight. It must have been a real fight
to call for as strong a word as " victor " in telling the result. And both of these words, " bat-

tle " and " victory " tell of a foe, and, more yet, that that foe has been fighting, and has been defeated.

And that great name of " Jesus " tells of another name, the name of a place, the name of an event, of an experience—Calvary. That is the great outstanding word in our Lord Jesus' life down here. That was the pitched battle of the long fight which really began back at the manger-cradle, and ran on through Nazareth, and through the three-and-a-half years of tireless service.

There the tempter did his utmost and his worst. There our Lord by His sacrifice upheld the righteousness of His Father, revealed the great love of His Father's heart, and forever defeated the evil one, loosening us from all his claim upon us. Those must be the two ringing keynotes in talking about the tempter. The very name of our Lord tells of him who has been defeated. And Calvary spells out the place and the time and the blessed fact of the tempter's defeat.

Our Ignorance of His Devices.

These simple talks about the tempter are to be wholly practical. We ought to know about our enemy if we are to resist him. I have no wish to go into any speculations, but only to bring such clear information from the old Book of God as shall make us stronger to resist temptation, and to lead a victorious, pure life.

Paul said to his own generation of Christians about Satan, " we are not ignorant of his devices." Probably that was partly due to Paul's own faithful teaching, and to their acceptance of the simple teaching of the old Book. It certainly cannot be said to-day of any considerable number of professing Christians. There seems to be far more ignorance of his devices than knowledge.

And as a result prayer is often powerless; the simple faith that takes God at His word is reckoned remarkable because so rare; Christian lives are entangled with things that actually help Satan, though doubtless all unconsciously, surely, in most cases; and our minds are full of such hazy, beclouded ideas about the evil one that our activities and praying are terribly hampered.

It is a strange and striking characteristic of the Church to-day that people commonly do not believe in the personal existence of Satan, and freely say so. It is supposed to be rather a sign of mental strength to doubt his existence, and rather evidence of an old-fashioned childishness to believe in his being and in his power. And this seems to be felt even more than it is expressed, though it is freely enough expressed.

The change in this regard has been very radical within, say, the past hundred years or so. That is, in the eighteenth century, Satan swung in too far in people's consciousness. They remembered him but forgot to remember his Victor at the same time. Things were ascribed to Satan which could be traced to natural causes and processes.

Now, we have swung clear to the other extreme. Doubt of his existence is freely and commonly expressed. One who knows his characteristics can easily detect his own cunning influence at work there. The very doubt of his existence becomes evidence of it. And he is so subtle that he is actually eager to have men doubt his existence for a while, if so be he can tighten his own grip.

It is of intensest interest to note, too, that this doubt exists only in Christian lands. It is only where the name of his Victor, and of his own terrific defeat, are so well known that such doubt is expressed. Surely his serpent-trail can be easily traced in this. Where his defeat is known, and so his own inherent weakness is known, he would have us doubt his existence, and so spike the guns of our resistance to him. Without doubt were he better known, he would be more heartily hated; I mean in practical ways hated, and fought and resisted, and utterly defeated all anew in the great name of his Victor.

It stands out in sharpest contrast with this that no such doubt is expressed or known in heathen lands.   There he is known, and dreaded, and even slavishly worshipped, because of his power.   His defeat is a thing unknown except where the Gospel has gone, and even there the knowledge is not full, nor practically effective, except in smaller part.

Three Sorts of Evidence.

I want to bring you now to a brief sketch of the tempter's career.   And in doing that I shall not touch any of the speculative legends and myths that are so common.   We want to gather up simply some of what God's own Word tells of him.

Will you notice keenly before we turn to the Book itself that there are three distinct ways of proving the personality of Satan: First of all is the Biblical.   We shall be referring to that constantly in these talks.   For those who are willing to accept the plain teaching of Scripture there is no need of going further.   For this Book plainly teaches both his personal existence, and his great activity and power.

But for those who are not content to accept these teachings there are two other independent sources of evidence.   And each of them is quite conclusive in itself, to the earnest, seeking man.

There is the philosophical evidence. That is to say, there is no power apart from personality. That can be put down as a purely philosophical proposition. There may be manifestations of power without the personality being seen or recognized. That is very common. There cannot be power apart from an intelligence originating and directing it. And certainly there is an evil power in the world. That is plainly felt and recognized everywhere. Now that presence of an evil power argues plainly the personality of an evil being actively at work behind the scenes.

There is still a third line of approach quite distinct from these two, and as irresistible in itself. That is the experimental, or the evidence that comes through experience. Let a man who has been yielding to temptation try to quit; let a man try to cut with the sin he has been indulging; and he will at once become aware that he has a real fight on his hands. He will become conscious of a real power attacking him with terrific force. About that the man himself will have no doubt. It will come with peculiar force, and drive, and cunning subtlety. It will hang on with great tenacity and persistence.

Thousands of men to-day are in the thick of that fight. As long as a man yields to evil there is no fight. But when he pulls away then the fight is on. And even though he trusts in the great Name above every name, and finds victory through that Name, as he always may and will, it is still a victory through fighting, real intense fighting, with jaw locked, and fist clenched, brow moist, and incessant praying. That man will not be troubled any more about the keen, intelligent, persistent personality of the evil one. And his undoubting consciousness will only grow more positive as long as he persists in the fight against evil and compromise in his own life, even though he may be blessedly conscious of the greater One who is within. The victory always comes through fighting.

In these talks together the reference will be almost wholly to the Biblical evidence as being quite conclusive and satisfactory.

The Bible Viewpoint.

Will you now turn to this Book of God for a little? The clearer light is in the New Testament. It really becomes the explanation of what is said in the Old Testament. In the light shed upon the Old by the New, the Old becomes full of clear teaching.

The last of the books, John's Revelation, contains the most explicit direct teaching. There we are plainly told that the serpent of Eden is Satan himself. There was a being working behind Eden's serpent, with all the characteristics commonly associated with that dreaded reptile.

The Gospels reveal the greatest Satanic and demon activity on record. There Satan and his whole world of attendant demon-spirits, are accepted as real beings, of real power. Our Lord plainly so believed, and so taught. His experience in the Wilderness, and without doubt in Nazareth before, and certainly through the three years and more after, leave no doubt, both of His belief, and the realness of his fight, and the sweet reality of His victory that marked every step of His way.

His teachings about Satan are very plain and clear. Satan is the determined foe of God, and of all that is good. He is the "prince of this world." He is conducting an aggressive warfare. The whole action of life is against him. And he is defeated. Every one who will resist and fight him is assured of victory.

St. Paul's letters are full of the same sort of information, as are also the other epistles. These men who stood nearest to our Lord, who did such tremendous working and fighting in their Master's Name and power, these early giants of faith and tireless service, and heroic suffering—these men have no question, nor doubts, about a personal devil. Their fighting was too real to admit of doubt. They fought at too close grips, hand-to-hand, for doubt to get in.

And they knew victory too, constant and unmistakable. That intensified their belief in the realness of the fight, and the one fought. The best cure for doubt here is fighting, real fighting; resisting, stubborn resisting, and steady-insisting on the will of Jesus, the victory of Jesus our Lord.

Now these simple plain New Testament teachings throw a flood of light on the allusions to Satan in the Old Testament. Go back to Eden fresh from the newer pages of Revelation, back to Job, to the twenty-first chapter of First Chronicles, and the one hundred and ninth Psalm, and the third of Zechariah, and you understand at once clearly who this personality is that works in such deadly ways, and with such stubborn hate. The New Testament makes one keener in detecting the serpent trail. And once our eyes are sharpened to recognize it, we can see it with startling plainness in the old pages of the Book, and in all the pages of the book of common life.

Owing to the Original Sources.

Let any one who would know the teaching of the Bible take a rapid but careful run through its pages, noting every reference to the enemy. Take sheets of blank paper and note down in regular order every text, writing out just enough of the words to bring to your mind at once what the passage contains. Leave a wide margin at the right hand side of the sheet for any notes you may want to make.

A good concordance will help much. Though the habit of wide continual reading of the Bible *by the page* is the real basis of all such research, and makes it easy, and makes it strangely fascinating too, and even more—makes your conclusions much more reliable because each passage is gotten in its setting. And the setting really gives the meaning of the words themselves. Trace out and put down every place referring to the names and titles of Satan, to demons and the devil. It is really not nearly as laborious a task as it sounds. And there is a real fascination about it.

Such a simple gathering together and grouping up of the actual statements of this blessed Word of God will not only radically change one's belief regarding this cunning enemy of ours, but it will do more. It will affect our lives, and consecration, and surrender, if we are indeed determined to be true to our Lord. It will affect our praying, it will make us do more claiming in our praying, more taking of definite things. Aye, it will do yet more; if we are determined to follow our Lord fully there will come to us a new inner consciousness of something, or somebody, who is resisting us, is trying to turn us aside, or trip us up.

And if we are courageous enough to keep steadily on, we will find the meaning of such a verse as, " Greater is He that is in you than he that is in the world." [1] The commentary of actual experience will flood that statement with a light that cannot be gotten in any book. You will be convinced down into the very roots of your being of this: that the " world " one is great, terrifically great; much too great for you to deal with alone.

But, greater, aye, greater is the other One. No dictionary definition can make anything like a satisfactory meaning of that word " greater." Those two words, " great," " greater," will stand out with a strange sharpness to your eyes. " Great "—that's the enemy; how great only he knows who resists. But—ah, that is a blessed " but "; all the gospel is in that " but "; all the power of a perfectly obedient Nazareth life, a sacrificial Calvary death, and a triumphant resurrection morning, are in that " but." " But greater " is He—the Victor. The intensity of your fight becomes the new underscoring of that word " greater." The only satisfactory way of spelling that word that will at all satisfy your heart is to spell it with a J and an E, and then S-U-S—Great!—Greater!!

But now for that brief biographical sketch. There are seven chapters in it. But each can be

[1] 1 John iv. 4.

made simple and brief that the whole may easily be held in mind together.

The first chapter tells of Satan's original state before he became Satan. That name belongs to a later stage, after his character had changed. Originally, as created by God in His great love, this prince was a being of rare personal beauty, of great wisdom, with mighty power, and high dignity of position. The teaching of the Bible here is chiefly inferential, but so clear as to leave no doubt as to the facts which the Holy Spirit is bringing to us through these pages.

Jesus' words: " I beheld Satan fallen as lightning from heaven," [1] give a world of clear inferential light on this first stage of Satan's career. Weymouth's translation, in the footnote, gives " a rendering less brief but more exact," in these words, " I was looking on when Satan was hurled like a lightning flash out of heaven." Taken with other scriptures this points clearly to Satan's early glorious history.

The Ezekiel Picture.

May I ask you to turn to a remarkable passage about Satan? It is in the prophecy of Ezekiel. There are three chapters dealing with the kingdom of Tyre, a Phœnician island-kingdom of ancient times, lying on the Mediterranean coast, north-west of Israel's territory.

[1] Luke x. 18.

Tyre was one of the greatest, most prosper-
ous, most powerful, most arrogant, and most
luxurious of the great kingdoms of the world
of its time. Of that much at least, we can be
quite sure. Probably much stronger language
could be correctly used. Ezekiel is talking about
all the great nations surrounding Israel. In
turn he comes to this kingdom of Tyre; and
chapters twenty-six, twenty-seven, and most of
twenty-eight, contain the Tyre message. It is
a message of judgment.

At the close of it occurs this most remarkable
passage—chapter twenty-eight, verses one to
nineteen. The first ten verses speak of " the
prince of Tyre," the next nine verses of " the
king of Tyre." The first is a message to the
prince, the second a lamentation over the king.
The title " prince," you will notice, is a subordinate or secondary title to " king." A prince
is under a king. A king rules over his princes,
who in turn may rule over those under them.

The language used here of the prince is such
language as can properly be used of a man.
Indeed, he is called a " man." The language
used of the " king " is not such as is ever used
of man, nor could it be so used. But it is most
striking that exactly the same spirit dominates
the prince as the king. The same characteristics strikingly mark each. The prince is an exact duplicate, a sort of understudy, of the king.

The same beauty, wisdom, and power mark each, and the same awful defiance of God breathes in both alike.

Remember that this Book of God is written from God's standpoint. It sees things on the earth as seen through God's eyes. This should be kept clearly in mind. The Holy Spirit seems to be giving us here a simple picture of the scene as it appears from *above,* to His own eye.

There is a man recognized among men as ruler of the kingdom of Tyre. There is another ruler, unseen by men, who rules the ruler of Tyre, and who so completely dominates him that this under-ruler perfectly carries out the purposes of his chief. Yet this prince of Tyre is one of the mightiest kings of earth of that time. The same classification would make all the kings of earth "princes" and this unseen spirit one of a higher order and higher rule.

It is a perfect illustration of thorough organization, the higher one, unseen by those on the scene of action, completely carrying out his own purpose through a subordinate. The second passage (verses 11-19) relates to the "king." It seems to give a simple sketch of this unseen master-spirit who rules this mighty, earthly king, and dominates him so absolutely.

The picture drawn of him at the beginning of his career is a most remarkable one, in its wisdom, beauty, and simplicity, and yet its strength.

He was not only beautiful in person and wise in rare degree, but, in language most striking as coming from God Himself, it says he was perfect in both beauty and wisdom, filling out the full measure of what was possible in both these regards.

He was in the most intimate personal relation with God Himself. Notice, " Thou wast the anointed cherub that covereth; thou wast upon the holy mountain of God; thou hast walked up and down in the midst of the coals of fire." Without going into how much those words mean just now, it clearly points to the closest intimacy and fellowship between God and this magnificent creature.

The Break with God.

That is the first chapter in this strange biography. Then follows the second: " Thy heart was lifted up because of thy beauty; thou hast corrupted thy wisdom by reason of thy brightness." " Unrighteousness was found in thee." " Thou hast sinned." Here is put simply the root of his sin, and you will note keenly that it is the root of all sin. His sin and ours are of closest kin.

He preferred himself to God. He thought of his beauty and wisdom as something that belonged to himself independently of God. And more yet, he thought of these as *for* himself, instead of being only for God, and His glory. They came from God, their source; they were dependent upon God, their life; they were for God, their purpose. Satan thought only of himself. The whole core of sin is here, preferring one's self to our wondrous Lover-God.

The words spoken by his underling, whom he has so dominated, puts yet more keenly the innermost purpose of his heart: "Thou hast said, 'I am a god, I sit in the seat of God'"; "thou hast set thy heart as the heart of God." "Wilt thou yet say, 'I am God'?"

This is the very core of sin. It is rebellion against God. It is dethroning Him, and taking the throne for one's self. It is nothing short of startling to find how common is this very thought about God and one's self. Rarely indeed is it put on human lips so plainly and bluntly and openly. But it is *lived* as truly as this old prince spoke it. And quickly upon the heels of that came the natural logical result: "I have cast thee as *profane* out of the mountain of God; and I have destroyed thee, O covering cherub, from the midst of the stones of fire."

Such is this striking Ezekiel passage, which came to the prophet as a word spoken by God Himself. It puts simply, and concisely, and clearly, the first two stages of this prince's career. First, the great beauty, rare wisdom and close fellowship with God Himself; then the sad break away.

Our Lord's thrice-repeated phrase,[1] "The prince of this world," suggests in this connection that this earth was the realm over which he was set as administrator. He seems to have been the rightful prince of this earth, but he has become the traitor-prince through being untrue to the trust; and the usurper-prince through seeking to retain control of the earth as his own dominion, through deceiving man, to whom the earth's dominion was given, into obeying him, and in utter defiance of God.

The third chapter of Satan's career is the present one, a very long one, beginning from the time of that break away, on through these centuries of our earth's history, and to continue until the close of the present order of things. His whole purpose is to swing the earth and man wholly away from God, and wholly for himself. In this chapter, two-thirds of the way on, occurs the great crisis of his present career —the stupendous event of Calvary, where his fate, so far as this earth and our race is concerned, was settled forever.

The fourth chapter is the one following this present time, when our Lord shall return to establish His kingdom, and Satan shall be

[1] John xii. 31; xiv. 30; xvi. 11.

" chained," in the simple language of the Book,[1] and kept in restraint for a long period, a thousand years.

The fifth chapter tells of his being " loosed again." [2] That seems very startling. It would seem that once he is securely fastened up he should nevermore be permitted any freedom again. But our God is a wondrous sovereign. He is a love-God. He wants our love, pure and glad, and freely given. That millennial kingdom will contain many who render only a " feigned allegiance." They go with the crowd and the current of their time, but at heart do not prefer God's way.

There is to be a final sifting time, a testing time. Those who at heart prefer the reign of this coming pretender-prince, and it is startling how many even within Church lines do, these will be given free choice to do as they prefer. Our God wants only a love-following, only heart-followers. And so the final testing time is allowed—an awful time of sifting.

Then will come the final chapter,[3] when the last crisis is over, and Satan is finally judged, and put away for ever and ever. Such is a brief story of the sad career, past and future, of this great spirit.

---

[1] Rev. xx. 1-3.   [2] Rev. xx. 7-9.
[3] Rev. xx. 10.

A Human Understudy.

It is both striking and startling to find that there is a human illustration of his career. There is portrayed for us, with great faithfulness in detail, by the Holy Spirit, the character and career of a man, who fills out with strange exactness, this strange story of Satan. It is found in the biography of King Saul of Israel. His career is put down for us in the Word of God, with that peculiar fidelity to truth in outlining human character, that marks this Book. That it is put down here for a real practical purpose, no one who reads carefully can question.

Notice please, very briefly, the story of Saul's life. It is all found within less than fourteen pages of First Samuel.[1] He was a man of unusual personal beauty, and excellence of character. He was chosen by God to be a Prince over His people. He was peculiarly endowed by the Spirit of God for this work. He ruled for a time with real rare wisdom, with great fidelity and obedience to God's purposes.

Then he acted independently of God; he preferred his own way, persisted in it, and defended it. He was set aside as God's chosen one. Another was chosen in his place, to be God's prince over his people. But he refused to transfer

[1] 1 Samuel ix.-xxxi.

the realm to his God-chosen successor, though he knew and acknowledged that this other one was God's own chosen one to rule in his place. He not only refused, but he fought his successor; he persistently and tenaciously and devilishly fought him up to the very end.

He was defeated. At the close of his career, in the sore plight in which he found himself, he sought the aid of demons, of evil spirits. Finally he died by his own hand. And then there is a startling point to mark at the very close; that is to say, it is startling when one thinks of the great rebellious spirit-prince of whom we are talking—namely, his successor grieved sorely over him in his death.

Yet he that knows the heart of God, as given so tenderly and fully in this Book, knows this, that while His purity flames out against sin, and He cannot do anything else than judge it, and burn it out, and burn it up, yet His great heart grieves sorely over His children, the sons of men, and over the higher spirits who have so sadly fallen.

Is not that a most striking parallel between these two princes: the first prince of Israel and the first and chief of all the princes of the upper world? But I am very sure there is yet more in the parallel between the stories of Satan and of Saul. There is something intensely personal to us. Saul perfectly produced in him-

self the career of Satan from the break on.   It
is possible for a man to reproduce the Satan
character.   A man may be a mirror reflecting
clearly and fully in his own life the characteristics of that traitor-prince.

Mark very keenly and prayerfully—the core
of all Satan's rebellion was his preferring himself to God.   He wanted his own way.   That
was all.   But that was terrific.   He was self-
willed, he persisted in his self-will.   Here was
the one seed, out of which his whole character
and career grew into their awful strength.   May
I ask you very softly, please, do you find any
of this sort of seed inside yourself?   Let the
answer be only to yourself, as all alone in God's
own presence, with this strangely searching
Word of His open, you find your inner motives
laid bare by the faithful Holy Spirit.

As we close our talk may we not very quietly
offer this petition in our hearts, and repeat that
great prayer of David's: [1] Search me, O God,
and know my heart; and let me know about this
heart of mine, what Thou dost know.   Try me,
and know my thoughts—that is, my innermost
motives, my undermost purposes, my hidden-
away ambitions—the thing underneath all else
that is really gripping my life.   Try me.

" Try " is a fire word.   It means a hotly
heated furnace, and the metal heated to the

[1] Psalm cxxxix. 23, 24.

liquid state, that all the dross may be freed out
and come to the top in clear view, and then be
painstakingly skimmed off. "Try me." It's
not an easy prayer to make. Yet it is the only
prayer that will meet the case here. "Try me"
—find out, and put out. Let the fire-test come.
Can you make that prayer? Aye, you *can; will*
you? There's a wondrous life of purity and
power at the end of that road.

And see if there be any way in me that
grieves Thee; and help me see what Thou dost
see; and help me be grieved over what I see
even as Thou art. And lead me—and here the
iron of one's will comes in—*lead* me; here I am,
willing to be led.

> "I was not ever thus, nor prayed that Thou
>   Shouldest lead me on;
>   I loved to choose and see my path,—but now—
>   Lead Thou me on."

Here I am, ready to go along as Thou dost
lead; lead me out of *this* way, into *Thy* way, *the*
way everlasting.

HIS AIM AND AMBITION

The Trinity of Action.

There's a new trinity that the earnest man wants to get hold of. At least it is new in not being much talked about. It is the trinity of action, the three that come into contact in the action of life, three persons in one action. The man who earnestly wants to win in the fight of life needs to know about this trinity of action.

If a man would be pure; if he would be strong; if he would make no partnership of any sort—silent or otherwise—with sin, he must fight. If he would keep that sly, subtle, stubborn thing called selfishness out, clear out and clean out, with no tail-ends left anywhere about; if he would keep humble, self-forgetfully humble, seeking nothing for himself, he must fight for it. If he would be free from that peculiar money-slavery, whose clanking chains are rarely out of sight or sound wherever one goes; if he would know the rare sweets of that rarest of all things, self-mastery, he will have to do some real, hard, stiff fighting.

The earnest man knows that life is a fight. The presence of the tempter makes it a fight.

The man's earnest purpose to be true, both to himself and to his Lord, brings the fight out, and brings it on, and makes it a very real fight so far as he is concerned. Now, such a man in the thick of the fight, wants to know about this new trinity if he is to be a keen fighter, and if he is to win in the fight. If he is not to suffer shameful defeat he must know about this three-in-one.

You know the fight of life may be settled in one of three ways. A man may be defeated. He may make an honest fight and be defeated; and a good many men are. Or, he may make a sort of truce, a compromise, a stand-off. He may agree not to fight, that is, not to oppose in any aggressive way the power of evil, but just to slip smoothly along, content not to oppose, but to play the part of a neutral.

Yet that is really the same thing as a defeat, only it is not a decent defeat; it is cowardly. There is no neutral ground, where right and wrong are involved. The man who fights, and is whipped has the comfort of knowing that at least he fought—he is not a coward. But this easy-going fellow has not enough heart to make a good fight. He's too diplomatic. Cowards are rare diplomats. It is surprising how many are letting the fight of life be settled in this slipshod way.

Then there is a third way, fighting *and win-*

ning. The earnest man will fight, *and* he may win, and he *will* win, if our blessed Lord Jesus may have His way in his life. Now, to know about this trinity of actions in the fight of life is an immense factor in winning. And the earnest man should know about it.

The first one I will name in this trinity is the tempter, the splendid spirit-prince of this world. I name him first because he is the aggressor. He started the fight, and he is forever keeping it up. I name him first, too, because we are living on the earth—and he is the prince of this world. This is the battle-field, and this prince is at home here. He knows all the ground well. He is fighting on familiar ground, and in that he has great advantage. The earnest man wants to get some clear, sane, workable information about him.

The Human Battle-field.

Then the second one in this trinity is the man himself. He is the real scene of the conflict. I said the earth is the battle-field and that is true. It is true because man is on the earth. It is our presence here that makes it the battle-field. This earth is ours as well as our present home. We were given mastery over all its riches and forces. It is our presence here that makes the fight. We men are really the battle-ground.

The tempter works upon us, and he works *through* us. He must work through us. It is his only way. Only as Satan gets control of men can he carry out his ambitions for the earth.

Every man is a battle-field, a spirit battle-field. Every man is being besieged. If the evil one be in control,—and it is startling, to the point of being painful, in how many of us he is in control, even where we are quite unconscious that it is he, for he is very adroit in keeping out of sight. If he be in control, then the Lord Jesus is laying siege, lovingly, tactfully, persistently trying to win His way in.

And wherever the Lord Jesus has been given mastery, the enemy is, by every artful device known to deceit, trying with malicious cunning and persistence to get in at some corner or crevice. But—*but* the man within is the deciding factor. The man settles who shall come in and rule his life. Every man's heart is his castle. There he is sovereign, and none can come in without his consent.

There is only one knob to the door of a man's heart. That is on the inside. The tempter cannot get in unless the man within turns that knob and lets him in. And, be it remembered with greatest reverence, that our gracious God *won't* come in except by the man's free consent. *Man* is the battle-field. He decides which way the bat-

tle should go. No man can be whipped without
his own consent. And every man may have victory, sweet and full, if he wants it. Man is the
second of this trinity of action, the middle one.
The thick of the action swings around him.

An Unfailing Ally.

And the third one is the Holy Spirit. His
place of activity just now is this earth. He
represents our Lord Jesus, and is clothed with
full power as His representative. When Jesus
was on the earth He yielded Himself wholly to
the Holy Spirit, and was entirely under His control. When He finished his work on earth, and
went back home again, the Holy Spirit yielded
Himself wholly to the control of our Lord Jesus.
And now He is here on the earth, the messenger
and representative of our Lord Jesus, clothed
with absolute power. He is the Lord Jesus'
other self, sent down to carry out His plans, and
to make real and actual in your life and mine
the *victory* which Jesus won for us when He
was here.

This is the great third One of this trinity of
action. It is He that so lovingly and persistently
lays siege to human hearts. He works wholly
through our wills. He will come into our lives;
he will take supervision of our temptations; he
will be the general on our side in every fight.

He gives us all the victory of Jesus over Satan. That victory, won years ago, He will make a present victory in your life and mine.

All this experience, and skill, and power, and the enormous prestige of a victory already won, He puts at our disposal. We can be as sure of victory as we are sure that our Lord is actually Victor. This Holy Spirit is our personal friend. He is always alongside, *inside,* to help. He devotes Himself to us. And in His presence we have all the power of God, and all the victory of Jesus, at our disposal in our life-fight.

This is the trinity of action—a real devil to be resisted and fought, a real Holy Spirit devoting Himself to us, and we men in between deciding the fight by our choices. We know that we men are real. We have no doubt about that. We know the conflict of life is a real thing. The earnest man has no question about that. Well, these other two are just as real, though unseen. We want to look not so much at the things that are seen, but through and beyond these, at the things and persons unseen. For these are the real forces.

There is a devil to be fought. And a keen tough fighter he is, too, but he has the enormous disadvantage of having known a crushing defeat.

There is a Holy Spirit, too, to take charge of

our fight, to fight with us and through us. He has never known defeat. He is the Spirit of Jesus, the Victor over the devil. He is with us. He will make real in us the victory of Jesus. His presence assures victory. But it is victory through fighting. The fighting is real, and the victory is just as real.

And in between these two we men decide the issue. The devil is the tempter. He is the aggressor. He has great power and subtlety. The Holy Spirit is the Helper. He is the Victor-spirit. He has far greater power than the tempter. He never fails. He is our personal friend. The result depends upon us. We are the tempted. We may be the helped. We must recognize and resist the tempter. We must recognize and claim the power of the Holy Spirit. Through Him there is unfailing victory for us. That is the trinity of action in the fight of life.

The Awe of Power.

Now it will help us greatly to recognize and resist the devil, if we know a bit more about him. Knowledge here will be a real help to power. I want to talk with you just now about his ambition and his aim. If we understand what it is he is aiming at, and what motive is controlling him, it will help us greatly in rec-

ognizing him when he approaches us under
cover.

It helps to note the difference between aim
and ambition. The aim is the purpose of one's
life; the ambition is the passion burning underneath. The aim is the thing you are driving at;
ambition is the thing you are driving with, or
the thing that drives you toward the aim. The
aim is the goal; the ambition the motive power.
The aim is the driving point; the ambition is the
driving power.

What are Satan's aim and ambition—the purpose and passion that control him? I think we
can get the answer quicker, and clearer, and
better, if we take a moment to note the effect
produced by the possession of power.

Power always has a peculiar effect upon those
who have it. That effect may be either good or
bad. Power either awes, or it itches. It produces a sense of reverence and of responsibility,
or it causes a sort of self-itch. That word
"itch" may not seem just a nice word to use,
but it is so accurate and graphic that I think
it helps to use it, that we may better understand.

Each of us has power of some sort, and in
some degree, some more, some less. It may be
the power that comes through the possesion of
physical beauty. Beauty gives power over others. It may be power through a keen mind, a

well-stored and well-trained mind; power of
personal presence and touch, of wisdom, of
leadership among men in the action of life;
power through what one can do; power through
the possession of money which is so enormous,
or power by reason of position official or otherwise. Now whatever sort of power it may be,
and in whatever degree it be possessed, it has
one of two effects upon us.

There is the good effect, the true effect that
it should have—it should awe. It all comes
from God. It is given us by Him. It is not
a thing that we possess of ourselves, simply.
It is a gift. That should awe and humble us, to think that God has given us such a
gift.

Then it is a trust. God entrusts it to us. We
are responsible to Him. We are trustees. No
matter what the power, it is something given us
by God in trust. As we realize this it makes
us yet more humble and prayerful, that we may
be true to the trust, and make the best use of
the gift for God.

And then it may be used among men. That
is the purpose in its being given to us. It is
for others. We are to use it for men's sake, in
God's name, to His glory. So God intended.
That is the threefold fact about any power that
you and I possess. And to realize this at all
makes one very thoughtful and prayerful that

it be used wholly as intended. The possession
of power awes—that is the true, the good
effect.

The Itch of Power.

Then there is the bad effect, where the hurt
of sin gets in. It itches. There is the itch of
thinking that you have it. You are pleased with
yourself. You are taken up with the fact that
you have the power. How beautiful you are;
how mentally keen; how well you do certain
things; how you can make men and things bend
to your desires; how a look, or a word, or a
finger uplifted makes things go. It may not be
expressed in so many words; it may even be hidden away under an outside of apparent humility, but you feel it; you know it; it is the
dominant thing underneath in your thoughts.
That's a bit of the itch of power.

Then, with that, goes the supposition or dis-
tinctive feeling that this power is from yourself.
It is really due to you. It originates in you.
That is the reason you are puffed up so big.
The " I " is printed so big as to belittle all the
other letters of the alphabet, even the letters
G, and O, and D. The Giver of it is forgot.
Mirrors are in demand here, especially the sort
that cast a rosy-hued glamour. The fact of
trusteeship has entirely slipped out of sight.

The upward look is lost; the inward look absorbs the eyes.

And then the swing over into the next stage is very smooth and easy. This power is to be used for yourself. The one passion here is how to use it all for your own advantage. There may be giving, or doing for others, but this is merely incidental, and the whole tendency is to make it seem as big as possible. The purpose underneath the giving or the doing, is to puff up the sense of pride, or else to get more for yourself in return.

These are the two effects produced by the possession of power of any sort; the good and the bad; the natural and the unnatural—the awing sense of God, and the itching sense of self.

This great spirit-prince has great power, power of beauty, of mental and spiritual endowments, and of position. They were given him by God as a trust, to be used for the Giver. The true aim of his life was to glorify God. That was God's purpose in so richly endowing him. He was to administer this world for God. He was to do just what our Lord Jesus will do when He returns to set up the kingdom upon the earth. In his own character, may I say very reverently, he was to be what our Lord Jesus was in His character. This was his true aim. The possession of the rare power entrusted to him was meant to awe, to fill him with a reverential love for the Giver, and an earnest desire to be true to the great trust reposed in him.

The true ambition underneath his aim was to be a tender, burning passion for God. The God-passion, the one dominant desire to please God—this was to be the one fire burning in his heart.

What is his aim? and what his ambition? They follow the line of the true, but with this startling difference, he puts himself in the place of God. The one aim of his life, mark it very keenly, is to get the world for himself! He would drive God out, and have all for himself. He would dethrone God, and take the throne himself. He would kill God off that he himself might be supreme.

It is with greatest difficulty that such words can be spoken or written. They seem blasphemous. They *are* blasphemous. His whole burning, driving aim is just that—blasphemous! Yet mark very keenly that it is a very common blasphemy in our common life.

Satan-Worship.

And the ambition underneath this aim is—himself. The self-passion burns so fiercely within him that all else is consumed in its flame. The shorter spelling of Satan is, s-e-l-f. The great passion of his heart is to be worshipped. And it is startling how far he has succeeded in having this passion satisfied. Devil-worship is very common in Africa, and in other heathen lands. There are said to be societies for devil-worship in Paris. But it concerns us to mark keenly that it is not needful to go either to heathendom or Paris to find Satan-worship.

For worship means the ascription of worth. And the Satan-spirit is simply the self-spirit, in some one of its numerous forms. And there is nothing commoner in all life than the self-spirit. Sometimes it is very cultured. It takes a very high polish. It sometimes wears saintly garb, and is skilled in the use of religious phraseology. Wherever that self-spirit, that self-seeking spirit rules the inner motive there is the thing Satan is after—the worship of himself. Imitation is the sincerest worship. It is not thought of in any such blunt fashion, of course. The very suggestion that any of us is indulging Satan-worship is repugnant.

And of course no one of us may say it of any other one. I am merely talking in this blunt way, and turning in this terrible searching light upon the Satan character, and the Satan characteristic, that you and I may go aside thoughtfully and prayerfully, alone with God, that we may see within what He sees. Satan really becomes a mirror for our use. As we talk over his characteristics, does there come up to our eyes anything of this same sort within? As his aim and ambition come out thus sharply, are you conscious, or maybe only half-conscious of something of the same sort within? Of course, not in such degree probably, and yet—— The truth is that no one of us can look into this picture of the evil one without being aware of the distinct resemblances between him, and certain characteristics within ourselves.

In some degree we know the very common thing called selfishness can be found within. It is shocking to find that this is simply the Satan-spirit. It is painfully searching to think prayerfully of these Satan marks and traits. It is startling in the extreme to think that we may have been helping Satan in any way; that he has been depending much upon us in furthering his ambitious aims. Yet every bit of selfishness in you or me spells out partnership with him. Selfishness, the self-spirit, the keeping for ourselves of anything that is not needful for strength, and that might be out in blessed service among men for our Master, that is the Satan-spirit. That is a footing for him in our lives. It not only means an emptying of our own lives of God's own presence and power, but vastly more and sadder than that—it is an active, positive help to Satan in achieving his aims. Satan is a mirror. He reflects to our eyes whatever there is of the same sort within ourselves.

The True Aim.

There is another mirror that this Word of God holds up to our eyes. It is the character of our Lord Jesus. I speak of Him because He and Satan are the two great claimants for our allegiance. They are the two great rivals. Our Lord's character here is revealed no better than in some words He spoke about Himself. And all men have agreed that what He said about Himself here is true. He said " I came . . . not to do my own will but the will of Him who sent me."

That was the undercurrent of his life throughout; in the commonplace Nazareth village, and home, and carpenter shop, through the years of tireless ministering to the hungry crowds, in the bitterness of the Gethsemane suffering, in the untold agony of the Cross. Like an undercurrent of music it runs through all His life. Sacrifice was gladly yielded to, pain was cheerfully suffered, even while the knife cut in deep— service was a delight, because in these He was carrying out His Father's plan.

The purpose of His life was to do His Father's will; the passion, the Father Himself. The gripping, controlling aim was the Father's plan; the burning ambition underneath, the Father—a tender love-passion for the Father.

This is the contrasting mirror held up to our faces. We might shrink from saying that this finds a reflection in us. And yet down in the inner purpose of the heart, that can be the one gripping, dominant thing. It has been the gripping, purpose-passion that has swayed His true followers in every age; and it is all by His wondrous grace. Wherever His Spirit is allowed to dominate this will be the gripping passion and purpose.

Please mark very keenly this, that one of these two characteristics dominates every man's life, either the Satan-characteristic or the Jesus-characteristic. The absence of the one tells of the presence of the other. By so much as our Lord's own purpose and passion do not control, by just that much is Satan in, and making use of us. This is simply the very old question of consecration or surrender from another standpoint—the Satan standpoint.

A Sensitive Thermometer.

Let the thoughtful earnest man look a bit at his inner motives from this point of view. Let there be no morbid spirit of extreme introspection, but a simple, wholesome look within. For example, there is no more sensitive thermometer than the money-thermometer, by which to find the degree of heat of one's passion for doing the Father's will. Let a man quietly alone ask himself how far the money he controls is being used as our Lord would have it used, *and* how far it is being used for himself.

Remember it is right to use some of it, a proper proportion for one's self and one's own; to do all that is needful for strength and comfort. Remember, too, that the passion of our Lord's heart is to have all men know fully and tenderly about His love and death for them; and that to-day two-thirds of them do not know anything about Him, and thousands of the other third know very little. I am not talking about the very proper thing of conscientiously giving a tenth of one's income. This question goes very much deeper—how far am I controlled in the money I control by the passion that controls my Lord's heart?

And of course the answer is not to be made to anybody else, but to one's self, and one's Master only. And that answer is not an answer of the lips. It is made entirely by what *proportion* of one's money is actually being used, or held, for one's self or one's own, and what proportion is being used in satisfying the burning passion of our Lord's heart for His world.

There are other thermometers that can be

used in taking the heart temperature. This is
only one. It is a very sensitive one. Perhaps
most times it comes nearest to telling how far
the warm love of our Lord's heart is affecting
the temperature of our own. By so far as the
passion of our Lord's heart is not dominant in
ours, by just that much is this traitor-prince
having use of us. It is a very searching question. It is not a question for any of us to
ask another, but only for each to ask himself,
or better yet to ask His Lord, off alone in the
secret place.

David's prayer might be brought into use
again, with a new meaning, in the light of this
subtle Satan-characteristic :—search me, O God,
and know my heart, and let me know what Thou
dost find there. Apply the fire test to my controlling passions and purposes, and let me see
how much dross Thou dost find there. See if
there be anything there that pains Thy heart,
and let me see as much of what Thou dost see
as I can stand; and—I wonder if one's courage
will stand the test of that closing petition—
lead me out of that way, into Thy way, the
Lord-Jesus-way, the way everlasting.

HIS DEFEAT

Satan is being forgot. That is the chief danger regarding him to-day among Christian people as well as others. He is ignored, even where he is believed in as an actual personality.

There is a feeling among earnest, godly people that this is a dreadful subject. Better put it aside, and go on doing the best you can in earnest dependence upon God's grace. The thought of Satan gives a feeling of dread, almost akin to horror. The result is a failure to get definite, clear thought about him, so as to resist him more intelligently and victoriously in the great Victor's great Name. Satan is practically ignored and forgot. That is very bad. It leaves him free to work. That is the most common danger to-day regarding him.

There is a second danger less common, but not less real; namely, that we shall think too much of him, when we begin to study the teachings of God's Word about him. Unless we are on our guard against it, there is an easy tendency to think that he is bigger and stronger than he is. That is bad, too.

Extremes are always bad, and work harm. We want to keep the poise between the two, though that is the hardest thing to do, and the rarest thing to find. He should not be minimized *nor* magnified. Clear outlines will let us see him as he is, neither smaller nor bigger. And this will be an immense help in *resisting* him, as we are bidden to do. Our resistance of him, in our Lord Jesus' Name, will become an immense factor in undercutting his activity and power.

There are two things that help immensely in correcting this second danger—the danger of being afraid of him, as we learn how real he is, and how tremendous is the power he wields.

The first is always to couple the Name of our Lord Jesus with Satan's, in all our thinking. Remember Satan, big, bold, cunning, sleepless, and quite too much for any one of us alone. We are clear outmastered by him at every turn. Don't get him in *too* big—nor too small, just the right size, as revealed to us in the Book.

But—*but,* remember Jesus too; He is bigger and stronger. He is more than a match for Satan. You and I are clean out-matched by Satan, out-classed and out-done; *but* Satan is clean out-matched by our blessed Lord Jesus, clean out-classed and out-done. We can't hold our own alone against Satan, and—blessed fact for us!—he can't hold his own for a moment against our Lord.

Always couple the two names. Satan—big and strong, wily and persistent and aggressive. Be wary of him—keenly, intelligently, earnestly wary of him. And Jesus—bigger to the point of being almighty, stronger, wise in conflict, resourceful in battle, and who undertakes for us. Remember Jesus, our Lord. That's the first thing that helps. The second is this, remember that Satan is *defeated*. We are fighting a defeated foe, who has all the enormous handicap of a defeat behind him. He *is* defeated, and he knows it.

Opening a Way for God.

We have the great advantage of fighting a defeated foe. All the stinging sense of defeat, the disappointment and disheartening that defeat makes he knows. And all the swing and spirit, the joyousness and elasticity of action, that comes from an assured victory already gotten, we have in our Lord Jesus. We ought to sing as we fight.

There is a fine, free reading of a verse in the Fiftieth Psalm that helps greatly in the thick of the fight. It runs like this, " whoso offereth the offering of thanksgiving glorifieth Me; and *openeth a way that I may show him the vic-*

tory of God." [1] That victory is already accomplished. Our spirit of thanksgiving (which is faith at its best) enables God to reveal all afresh in our lives the victory already won for us!

Sing as you fight. Pull out the organ stops and loosen the swells, and let the cheeriest, most joyous music of heart and voice out. For our enemy is defeated. Our Lord, our Friend, is Victor. And our resisting shall make his defeat more marked, and make it a more real thing in our own lives, and in our service among others.

It seems just a bit strange to be talking about fighting when the foe has been decidedly defeated. A decisive, overwhelming defeat of the chief of forces usually settles a conflict. There is a reason, and we will talk together about that in our next talk. Just now the fact we want to mark down big is that our tempter is fighting us against the heavy odds of a stinging defeat.

We can understand that defeat better if we will note the difference between the Satan-spirit and the Jesus-spirit.

The core of the Satan-spirit is this,—self, pride,—which is the assertion of self, the sense of inner satisfaction with yourself; conceit and egotism, the undue sense of one's own im-

[1] Psalm l. 23.

portance, and with that always, independence of
God. The feeling of one's own sufficiency always makes us feel independent of God, that
we do not need Him, and can get along well
enough by ourselves, by depending upon
ourselves.

The selfish spirit not only ignores God, but
it ignores the needs of others. Luxury is a
direct outcome of the Satan—the selfish spirit.
Whatever adds to our strength is properly
classed as a necessity. All beyond that is luxury. The self-spirit always breeds luxury. Yet
luxury always spells out somebody else's need
unsupplied. Every bit that is being kept for
ourselves, beyond the line of what will make
us stronger in body and mind, speaks out the
crying need of the great crowds who make up
the majority of our race. We hold for ourselves what we do not need, while two-thirds
of our brothers of the race are perishing in
their need of the Bread of Life. This is essentially the self-spirit, it is the very core of the
Satan-spirit.

The Spirit that Won.

In sharpest contrast with this is the spirit
that controlled Jesus when living His human
life among us. It was a spirit of selflessness, a
spirit of utter self-abnegation. He did not go

to the unwise extreme of neglecting what was needful for His strength as a man. He surely did not over-use His strength though that was one of His constant temptations, as with the man now who feels the needs of others pressing in so sorely upon him. For the sake of these multitudes He conserved His strength that He might minister to them the better. The whole spirit of His life was for others.

And underneath that was something deeper, explaining that. He had a passion for the Father. In the place of the passion for self was the God-passion. And if you will mark it very keenly this was revealed most in the obedience of His life. This is the very inner heart of the Jesus-spirit—obedience. This was the one unfailing warp into which all the cross threads of His earthly life were woven.

Cut in underneath at any point in His character, and this is the controlling motive. He reveals His passion for the Father in this— His glad, full obedience to the Father, no matter what it meant. The obedience reveals the passion. The passion found its full expression in the obedience. That passion and obedience were revealed much in the Nazareth life, but most on Calvary. The obedience was not simply in life, but unto death, even the worst sort of death that could be devised, with all the horrible cruelties and indignities that sin could think of. The sacrificial spirit is the very heart of the Jesus-spirit. Not seeking sacrifice, but yielding to it, as it comes in the pathway of obedience.

This is the innermost spirit of the Jesus-spirit—the passion for the Father, which leads to utter self-obliteration in the good sense, in a life of glad obedience, even to the point of keenest suffering and severest sacrifice.

This sharp contrast between these two spirits will help us to understand the defeat of Satan, how crushing it was, and further it points out the way on *our side,* and the only way whereby he can be defeated on the battlefield of each of our lives.

Defeated by a Life.

Satan was defeated by our Lord Jesus. There were two steps or stages in that defeat. The first was in the life He lived. That life ran through thirty-three years and a bit more. It was a long battle, and the defeat administered was all the more conclusive, and sure, and crushing, because of its length.

First of all came that Nazareth life. The one word that marks that Nazareth life, and sums it up, is the great, simple word "obedience." From the early, tender years, when the consciousness of His mission first began to come

to Him, on through the years of growth and
maturity, He obeyed. He insisted on obeying.

Jesus insisted on going that daily commonplace routine: white-washed cottage home, companionship with his fellow-workmen and fel-
low-villagers, long hours in a wood-working
shop, driving nails, pushing a plane, mending
ploughs and yokes for customers hard to please
sometimes. That was the Father's plan for His
life. He obeyed, because it was the Father's
plan. If the Nazareth round be put in sharp
contrast with the conditions to which the Son
of God was accustomed in His Father's presence—His intense humility stands sharply out.

Did no temptation come to Him those Nazareth days to quit that retired humble round
and go forth to let men know who He was, and
why He had come? Look at Him a moment
in Nazareth. He is, say twenty-eight years of
age, in the maturity of His human strength as
a man. Yet He goes the old humble commonplace round in that shut-away village, in the
little narrow-walled cottage home, rising early,
helping about the home, then down the street
with a cheery " good-morning " to neighbour
and fellow-craftsmen, then the carpenter shop,
mending a table, smoothing up carefully the
handle of a plough, at it for long hours, then
home again for the frugal meal, with the small
familiar talk of a home circle around a table.

Then likely as not talking over with the mother of the home the ever present problems of house-keeping, figuring out the slender funds to meet obligations, and so on, and so on.

Does any one of you think that no such temptation as this came subtly stealing in those days: " what are You doing *here* in this shut-away corner. You are the Son of God! (no 'if Thou be' then) You have a mission to the whole world; it is such a needy world too; so needy. You are to redeem a *world*. This is no place for You; assert Yourself, as the Son of God, for the good of the world."

Did no such insinuating voice speak such words in His ear? No one who knows the tempter can doubt it. But faithfully, steadily, obediently He went the old round up to the very last, when the Father's voice sent Him forth. The one touch-stone of His life was obedience to His Father's plan.

A Running Fight.

In that obedience He was cutting straight across the character and life of the traitor-prince of this world. He was holding the title to all the Father had given Him by His obedi-ence. He was undermining Satan's hold upon the race and the earth. His obedience was the defeating of Satan.

The one temptation, that came in a thousand differing ways, was to turn aside, if only by so much as a hair's breadth from the Father's will. The one answer was unflinching, unfailing obedience. And in that He was laying the foundation for the final defeat of the traitor-usurper-prince.

In His Nazareth life our Lord reveals His utter humility, His rare simplicity, His warm sympathy with men, and His spirit of sacrifice for others. And each of these is in direct contrast to the character of Satan.

But the chief thing underneath all the rest, the thing that controlled Him was the obedience to His Father's plan for His life. That was the basis of the defeat of the evil one. If Jesus had diverged by so much as a hair's breadth, the tempter would have been victorious. By remaining true He was defeated so far.

Then follows the great Wilderness temptation. His public ministry was prefaced with this terrific, though subtle, onset by the tempter. But again, our Lord held true and steady to the Father's will. The touch-stone of the Nazareth life is the touch-stone of the Wilderness victory, namely, full obedience to the Father's will and the Father's time. The Wilderness temptation ended in victory for Jesus—and so in defeat for the tempter.

And following that came the three years and

a half of public ministry. They were years of temptation, subtle and stormy, of attack in every conceivable shape by the enemy; of sharp struggle and conflict with the evil one and his forces. Behind demons, behind human leaders, even behind ignorant friends and followers, the enemy came, ceaselessly, day and night, doing his best and his worst, with his subtlest devices and his greatest resources.

It awes one greatly to draw near our Lord at certain stages, and note by the tensity of His spirit, how fierce the onset was. One can almost hear the deep-drawn breathing, and see the moist brow, and the firmly locked jaw, and hear the earnestly breathed prayer.

He never flinched and He never failed. He was a Victor at every step, by His full following of the path marked out for Him. And His victory spells out the defeat of the tempter. Each advancing hour of continued, steady ongoing was a deepening and intensifying of the defeat of the tempter. So our Lord defeated Satan in and by His life.

The Climax.

Then came the climax—the defeat in His death. Jesus was obedient not only in life, but even to the terrible experience of death, aye, the most shameful and cruel of all deaths, the

death of the Cross. He was first of all obedient in His life on earth, then He carried that
obedience right on into Satan's own domain,
the domain of death. He hesitated not to die,
though death was never made so dreadful
and awful a thing before, nor since. If Jesus
would insist on obeying even to the point
of death then Satan was set on it that He
should know the worst that could be known
in death.

By His death He did a three-fold thing and
that tells of the three-fold defeat of Satan.
Through sin Satan had done three things. He
cast a blot on God's administration of the uni-
verse; on the perfect righteousness of His rule.
Sin is a slander on God's righteousness. He
got a claim upon men who in sinning yielded
allegiance to the tempter and so became his
slaves; and he hardened the human heart
against God.

Our Lord's death smote Satan hip and thigh
at each of these points. He vindicated the
righteousness of God, He forever freed us from
the slavery of Satan, and He melted our hearts
by such a wondrous love. The man whose heart
is broken by such love comes back home to God.
And because of the death of Jesus, God is
" reckoned righteous in reckoning righteous the
man who has faith in Jesus." [1] And the hold

[1] Romans iii. 26, free translation.

upon us which our sin gives to Satan is forever shaken off. In His death Jesus administered a defeat to our enemy on every side.

And as the death was the climax of the life,
even so the resurrection became the climax of
the death. And our Lord of His own accord
went down into the jaws of death, into the
belly of hell on our behalf, in our place, as our
substitute; then having fully defeated Satan by
that act, He rose up by His own will, up again
into life. In His death He was Victor over
sin. In His rising again He was Victor over
death. In both He was Victor over Satan.

And every spelling of that word "victory"
is a spelling in big letters of the word "defeat."
Loosen all the bell-ropes. Ring out the bells
clear and loud. Our enemy is defeated. Pull
out the organ stops, free the swells, and let
the joyous thunder of the full diapason get out.
Our Lord Jesus *is* Victor. Our enemy is a
badly whipped foe.

The Second Defeat.

Then there is the second defeat. But, you
say, why a second? That question has an intensely practical bearing on your life and mine.
The first defeat was on the battlefield of the
earth. The second is to be on the battlefield
of each man's life.

Every man decides his own life and settles the outcome of his own battles by the way he chooses. Every man is a sovereign in his own will. What our Lord has done *for* us, we must each accept and claim for ourselves. Our Lord defeated Satan on *our behalf*. We must each of us claim all the power of that defeat on the battlefield of our own lives.

Jesus taught us to pray, " lead us not into temptation, but deliver us from the evil one." *He* was led up to be tempted, and He was victorious in the temptation. We men have been tempted, and failed. But in Jesus the Victor's Name, we claim His victory in our temptations. We cannot stand being tempted. Eden proves that, and every man and every day since Eden makes it plainer. We can't stand temptation *alone*. We must go in Another's strength, and in Another's victory.

" Lead us not " means that we get in close behind our Victor, and claim what He has done for us. But each of us must do that. With greatest reverence let it be said that our Lord Jesus cannot decide my battles, my temptations for me. He wins the victory for me. Then I must claim that victory in my own firm decision to resist the evil one.

The second defeat is to be on the battlefield of my will, in the power of the Lord Jesus. And that defeat may be just as radical and sweeping in my life, as it was on the Cross, and the resurrection morning.

May I close this simple talk by putting, in a brief word, how that defeat may become a real thing to me every day? First of all by trusting in the blood of our Lord Jesus. We overcome on the ground of the blood of the Lamb.[1] We hide ourselves in Him, and claim all the power of His victory, for ourselves in our conflict.

Then there must be the full glad surrender of life to the mastery of our great Victor-Friend. That means the recognizing and yielding to the gracious sovereignty of the Holy Spirit at every turn, in every act, until it becomes as habitual as breathing.

It means that there will be the same obedience, the same self-forgetting humility, the same tender, loving sympathy with men, the same simplicity of life, the same glad willingness to sacrifice for the needs of others, as marked our Lord's Nazareth life. This will be the standard habitually kept before the eyes of our spirit. For the Holy Spirit works out in us the life and spirit of our Lord Jesus.

Then there is something else on the Satan side of things. We should become keen in *recognizing* him. Recognition of temptation is half the fight against it. And with recognition

[1] Revelation xii. 11.

must follow resistance, quick and sharp. Resist the devil and he will flee from you.[1] He knows that he is defeated. He knows that he can't stand up before Jesus' victory. As we resist steadily he must leave, and he will, slowly, angrily, but surely before the power of Jesus' Name.

Resist Satan actively and aggressively. Learn to recognize his step and voice, and tricky devices, and then put up an earnest fight in the Victor's Name, and Satan will know his second great defeat on the battlefield of your life.

[1] 1 James iv. 7; 1 Peter v. 8, 9.

HIS PRESENT STRUGGLE

Each one must choose.

Every man must make his own decisions. No one can make a choice for another. Every man must do his own thinking.

We can accept another's choice for ourselves, but that is simply accepting the other's help in making the choice. We still choose to take his choice as our own. Another could not choose for us unless we were willing. That is, of course, where there is no force or coercion used, but every man free to act as God intended he should. Just as certainly every man must do his own fighting, and lose or win the fight.

With the greatest reverence let it be said that God cannot make decisions for us. With the same reverence be it said, too, that not even our Lord Jesus can fight our fights for us. He can put all of His power, and all the advantage of His sweeping victory at our disposal. But we must choose to accept and use. He works *through* us. So working He makes our victory as full and sure and sweeping as His own,

by placing His strength at our disposal. Every
victory won is by His strength through our own
wills.

This explains why there should be a present
struggle going on by Satan. It seems strange
that after a defeat, the defeated is left free
to fight. Defeat, of as radical and crushing and
sweeping a sort as Satan has suffered at the
hands of our Lord, usually means a settling of
the conflict at once and forever. But here is
a strange and striking exception. Satan has
been defeated, but he has been and is fighting
as hard as ever, apparently, and with tremendous results for himself. Why is this? The
question is an intensely practical one, or I
certainly would not bring it up, here. For in
the thick of the fight there is only time and
spirit for the intensely practical. And the answer is tremendously practical, because the
whole matter is thrown over upon our action.

It is because of *us,* that the fight continues.
Were it not for us men, and the part we have
in this thing, Satan's activity would have been
summarily settled long ago.

The core of the answer is gotten at once by
noticing that our Lord Jesus was acting for us.
His whole life as well as His death was on
our behalf. It was for our sakes that He
came down to this earth, and lived as He did,
and was tempted, and suffered, and died. His

whole thought was to do something in our place.

It was something in which we had sorely failed. Our failure cost us, and lost us, mastery of ourselves, and the dominion over nature. It brought us suffering and death. It cut us off from God. It makes us slaves of Satan.

We have only what we take.

Jesus came to get us out of our awful plight. He came to the earth because we were here, and it was our home, our lost heritage. He lived His life of perfect obedience on the earth, because the earth had been lost to us through our disobedience. He would win it back through obedience, but He would win it back for *us*. All through He was acting in our place, as our substitute and representative.

But again be it said that He cannot do for us what we do not want. That is, He can't make us accept what He has done for us, unless we choose to. No one can make a choice for another nor act in the stead of another, but by the other's consent.

He defeated our enemy. He won back our lost dominion of the earth. He has won for us freedom from all the power of Satan, the power we gave him through our sin. But the results of His great victory become ours only

as we accept and appropriate them as our
own.

Each man of us may have His victory as our
very own. But it does not become our very
own until we accept it so. And so Satan, who
left Jesus when he must, will not leave us till
he must; and then, as with Jesus, "only for a
season." [1] Our sin gives Satan a grip upon us.
He insists on that grip.

And Satan has a right to us for we have
given ourselves to him by obeying him. For
sin is obeying Satan. So we become his slaves,
and he our master. He can hold that grip upon
us until a stronger than he comes along to worst
him. That stronger One has come—our blessed
Lord Jesus. But we must accept His victory
as our very own, and give Satan notice of
our decision. He must leave when he is
ordered off in the Name he fears. And he
will leave.

But he never leaves until he must. And so
there is a present struggle, even after an absolute defeat, because so many men have not accepted as their own what our Lord Jesus has
done for them.

Satan must be doubly defeated. First by one
stronger than he. That has been done by Him
whose very Name—Jesus—tells of victory.
Then he must be defeated by each one of us,

[1] Luke iv. 13.

on the battlefield of our own wills, by our choosing Jesus as our own representative, as our own Substitute-Victor.

In His Name and strength we can administer that second defeat. In no other way can it be done. And in His Name we must. As men, as rightful under-masters of this earth, as rightful children of our Father, who made us in His own image, we must defeat the evil one in the Name of Jesus, by choosing Him as our Saviour and Lord.

The struggle with our Lord was for the mastery of the earth, and the whole race. In that Satan has been defeated. The present struggle is for the mastery and control of each man's life. Our Lord won the victory over our enemy; now He would win His way into each man's heart and life.

Satan has been defeated on the earth, and on behalf of the whole race; now he must be defeated on the battlefield of each man's life. The first struggle was settled decisively by our Lord. The second can be settled only by each one of us, in the power of our Lord's victory for us.

The Real Struggle.

Then there is a second practical answer to that question of why Satan has power to con-

tinue his struggle, and it is rather a startling
one. The man who accepts our Lord Jesus'
victory as his own, must choose to let the Jesus-
spirit *control his life.*

If there be some part of my life uncontrolled
by that Spirit, that uncontrolled part is held
by Satan. Any bit of selfishness allowed to remain becomes Satan's footing in my life. He
holds that bit of ground stubbornly. And he
can hold it, for I yield it to him in letting the
selfishness or the wrong spirit remain. On that
ground he stands and struggles for more, so
there is a present struggle because I let him
have part control within.

If my Master has asked me to sell a bit of
property, whose income I don't really need, and
to send the money out through my church chan-
nels, that men in China may learn of the victory of the Lord Jesus—if so, and I simply
don't, that disobedience, that bit of self-will, that
bit of Satan-spirit, gives the evil one a fresh
hold upon my life.

In that I neutralize the victory of Jesus. I
am helping Satan in his present struggle. In
so far as your life and mine are not swayed
and swept by that Jesus-spirit of which we have
spoken, in just that far we are strengthening
Satan in his present struggle.

I will not stop to make a survey of the Christian world, and attempt to gather up into words,

how much help of that sort the cunning enemy is getting to-day from those who profess to belong to Jesus Christ. The results would be startling, and would without doubt seem critical, and in a bad way, even though merely a colour-less statement of facts.

Each of us would better go off alone, and look within, with that " search me " prayer, and with a willingness to look honestly at what that searching eye of God reveals within.

There is still another bit to be put in here. It is this; our ignorance of Satan and his wily ways of working is helping him greatly in his present struggle. Knowledge is power. Igno-rance is weakness. Our ignorance of Satan adds to his power immensely.

Satan is being strengthened in his present struggle because of the very common wide-spread ignorance of him. He works freely among us, and even—startling though it sounds —he works *through* us, yes *we Christians,* be-cause we have not learned to recognize his pres-ence, and so do not aggressively resist him in the Victor's Name.

We should remember that one of Satan's peculiar weaknesses is this—*he is dependent very largely upon our human co-operation.* Per-haps he is wholly dependent upon us men. His very first attempt in Eden was to get the con-trol of a human being, and once in control he

used that one to get another, and so on end-
lessly ever since.

If we men were to throw off his allegiance at
once in the power of the Victor, Satan would
not only be terribly weakened, but far more, he
would be driven out of his present sphere of
activity. He is dependent upon us in his present struggle. And right well he knows it. What
a soul-winner he is! With what persistence
and tenacity he keeps after a man who is trying
to get away from him!

The Battlefield.

This leads up naturally to the sphere of Satan's activity. Where is this great struggle
going on? Will you note that there are five
places of residence or head-quarters of activity
assigned to Satan in God's Word? First of
all he was in the presence of God.[1] After his
fall, he was cast out of that presence; his head-
quarters were moved to some place below the
throne of God, and above the earth, as the chief
sphere of his activity and ambition.[2] That is
his present scene of action, and will be until
the close of the present order of things.

After a while he is to be cast down to the

---

[1] Ezekiel xxviii. 13-17.
[2] Ezekiel xxviii. 16; Luke x. 18; Ephesians ii. 2; vi. 12.

earth.[1]   Then follows the time when he shall
be cast into a place called the "abyss" or
"pit";[2] and afterwards he is to be consigned
to what is called "the lake of fire."[3]   Our practical concern just now is wholly with his present head-quarters and sphere of activity.

His head-quarters is somewhere above the
earth; the sphere of his activity is the earth and
the atmosphere that envelops it.   His titles
"prince of this world,"[4] "prince of the powers
of the air,"[5] "the god of this world"[6] indicate
that.   The two great temptations in which he
himself was chief actor were on the earth, in
Eden, and in the Wilderness.

In the attack upon Job, two of the disasters
that came were war—an evil spirit aroused
among men—and two of them were wild storms
in the atmosphere that surrounds the earth.

In the remarkable story of Daniel, tenth chapter, the opposition to Daniel's prayer was by
some evil spirit-being, who intercepts God's messenger on his way from God's presence down
to where Daniel was on the earth.   While the
old man was praying on his knees in the woods

[1] Revelation xii. 7-9.
[2] Revelation xx. 2, 3.
[3] Revelation xx. 10.
[4] John xii. 31; xiv. 30; xvi. 11.
[5] Ephesians ii. 2.
[6] 2 Corinthians iv. 4.

down by the river Tigris, two spirit messengers, one from God, the other opposing God's messenger, and so from the enemy's camp, were wrestling up in the spirit realm above the earth. But the wrestling was regarding something down on the earth.

The very striking passage in Mark's Gospel [1] makes yet clearer the sphere of activity. A great storm had arisen while our Lord slept on a pillow in the hinder part of the boat. It must have been an unusually fierce storm to have so thoroughly frightened these old sailors. In distress and alarm they awaken Jesus and ask for His help. Notice both His action, and His words. The usual reading is He " rebuked the wind, and said unto the sea, Peace be still." The more literal reading is immensely suggestive and helpful. " He said to the sea, Lie down, be muzzled." It is the sort of language one uses in speaking to a dog that is misbehaving. If the word be repeated in the sharp peremptory tone of command, in which one speaks to his dog, it makes the sense yet more intense and real;—" down sir! lie down!"

The whole passage is significant. It is not the sort of language to be used in talking merely to wind and wave, especially by as even-poised a man as our Lord was. There is at once the recognition of an evil spirit, or a group of

[1] Mark iv. 35-41.

them, who had aroused the unusually violent storm.

The very language used is a recognition of personality. There was some one at work through wind and water. He is ordered down. He obeys. There was a great calm. But the point to mark just now is that his sphere of action includes wind and water as well as the earth. Mark keenly why this is the sphere of his activity—because we are here. It is us he is after, and through us the dominion of this realm.

Proper Air Supply.

You and I are living on the battlefield. We are in the thick of the engagement now on. We must take sides. And the side we take affects the result of the struggle, because that struggle is through us.

You know how a diver working down at the bottom of a river or of the sea, must take his own atmosphere along with him. He is working in a strange element—water. He must have his own native element—air—to live in and he must have a constantly fresh supply of it, too.

The prince of the power of the air has been tampering with the moral atmosphere of the earth; he has poisoned it. An atmosphere of

doubt, of compromise, of disloyalty to God surrounds us. We have to stay here and fight, and
it is hard work fighting in such air. Indeed
it is impossible. We must live in an inner air-
chamber, filled with the sort of air which is native to us. And that inner air-chamber must
have continual connection with the pure air of
God above.

Shall I give you a formula for the sort of
atmosphere for the inner air-chamber of our
lives? It is a simple formula with five items
in it. No one item can be omitted. First is
this, " the blood of Jesus cleanseth from all sin."
Second, is this—the whole of one's life and activities yielded to the control of the Holy Spirit.
Third, this—habitual obedience to His Voice.
Fourth, this—daily quiet time with the Book
that the ear may be keen to know what He is
saying, and the mind instructed in His will.
And fifth—recognition of the enemy, and earnest aggressive resistance in Jesus' great Name.

PERSONAL CHARACTERISTICS

Watch as well as pray.

One of the settled maxims of military wisdom is this—"study the enemy." Millions are spent annually by the governments of Europe and America, and, lately, of the Eastern world, in just this thing. Yet they go just a step farther, for they spend the money studying the military strength and tactics of nations that are now friendly, but that *may become* enemies. The general who would enter upon a conflict, without doing his utmost to learn everything possible to be learned about the enemy he must meet, would be regarded as greatly lacking in wisdom, if indeed he were not plainly called a fool.

Our enemy is not a *possible* enemy, but a real one. The war is actually on. And plainly God meant us to know about the enemy, for He has given us so much clear information about him and his forces, in His Word. Our Lord Jesus said, " watch and pray that ye enter not into temptation." [1]

The temptation is here. It reveals the tempter

[1] Matthew xxvi. 41.

in ambush. " Pray " is not enough. " Watch " is not enough. The two must be coupled. The eyes must be joined with the knees. And keen-trained, practised eyes they must be too. The " watch " is for the enemy, the " pray " for God. We must look out as well as look up. There has not been too much praying, but there has been far too little watching. While some of us have been devotedly absorbed in kneeling, the enemy has slipped in, and toppled us over.

We must learn to pray with our eyes open, and our ears alert, for our cunning enemy is lurking around. Praying that is not accompanied by watching is weakened. The knees need the eyes. The eyes watching the enemy will make the knees stronger in their work. Watching will reveal our danger, and make us realize more keenly the need of prayer, and of claiming our Lord's victory.

More watching would make more praying. We would feel more keenly the danger, and our own helplessness. Keener watching—eyes trained to see in the dark, would make keener, steadier praying. For we would realize more, how great the prayer is that can affect and up-set such an enemy as our watching brings into the light.

Our watching is hard on the enemy; he must fight harder. And our praying becomes more simple and definite, steadier and more quietly tense. And watching makes easier praying; it reveals to us our utter helplessness in ourselves alone, and then we throw ourselves on our Victor, and rest our case there. We can do nothing else before such a foe. And as we lean wholly upon our Defender, we learn to *rest* upon Him in our sorest straits. And that helpless resting upon His makes the results quicker and surer. Faith rests because of its very helplessness.

Some important " Nots."

Now that we may get our eyes trained for keener watching I want to talk with you a bit further about the personal characteristics of this tempter-enemy of ours. We want to know more about him so as to recognize and resist him better.

He is a being of great personal beauty, and with that goes the thought of great attractiveness. Yet it must be noted keenly that it is a spoiled beauty. Nothing mars like selfishness. The more beautiful face may become the most ugly. Sin makes ugly. Satan's beauty has been sadly spoiled, until now it is the false beauty of powder and paint, of gaudy dressing and flashy colours. He comes in a guise of beauty and attractiveness. He has enormous power, and real great dignity. We are told that

Michael in dealing with him on one occasion spoke respectfully, as to one in a position of dignity and glory.[1]

He is at the head of a vast compact organization of spirit-beings. Paul's description of this organization reveals how thoroughly disciplined and organized are the forces at his disposal.[2] And however the spirit of lawlessness and disregard for authority may permeate all his ranks, there yet is a dominant organization maintained and recognized, for so their purposes can better be achieved.

Paul says our fighting is " against the principalities, against the powers, against the world-rulers of this darkness, against the hosts of wicked spirits in the heavenlies." The words of highly endowed beings. Satan's personal character is revealed in such a compact organization, the creation of his skill, and being wielded by him.

But, over against that there are certain words to be put down in blackest ink. They tell at once of his limitations. He is *not* omnipotent, though the power he wields is greater than any of us realize. He is *not* omnipresent, though the superb organization at his command has sometimes seemed to suggest something of the sort. He has *no* fore-knowledge, though he is a very shrewd guesser. And he is *not* om-

[1] Jude 9.   [2] Ephesians vi. 12.

niscient, or knowing all things, though he has gathered great knowledge through the centuries. These traits belong to God only.

Indeed, in contrast with these, it should be said again that he is wholly dependent upon the co-operation of men so far as our lives and the earth is concerned. This is a bit of his inherent weakness.

And, further, a vast deal of the power he does have among us men, he has wholly, either through our foolish ignorance and ignoring of him or through our active (though I think largely unconscious) co-operation with him by the selfishness and sinfulness and compromise in our lives.

His Mental Status.

He is credited with having great intellectual keenness and force. He is thought of as a giant of intellectual power. And there must be much truth in such a supposition. The story of his creation, his close fellowship with God in his early history, and the work entrusted to him would all lead to the conclusion that his mental acumen and resourcefulness must be very great. This should be carefully noted.

Yet there is a bit of vast import on the other side of this fact. There is very much to lead us to believe that his mentality is distinctly of a *secondary-grade*. His is not a first-grade mentality. This should be noted, for it has great bearing upon our dealings with him.

Note, please, that he has great cunning and craftiness. His keenness is so great as to make one feel uncanny. He has a peculiar quality of persistence, and enormous driving power. Indeed these are his dominant traits mentally. Yet note that animals have great cunning and craftiness and keenness and persistence and energy. These do not indicate a first-grade mentality. Yet they are Satan's dominant traits.

Certainly he is not *wise*. That quality could not be ascribed to him, and it is a peculiar thing to mark that he constantly reveals a defective judgment. He constantly overreaches himself, and defeats his own purposes in dealing with us. This suggests that he is more of a shrewd guesser, with long experience back of his guessing, than anything else. A vast lot of what might be thought of as keen thinking, and as indicating wide knowledge or fore-knowledge, is simply very shrewd, crafty guessing.

Note that his dominant mental trait is imitation. He has been called "the ape of God." Read through Saint John's Revelation, and note how in everything he does there he is simply imitating God. There is a trinity of evil. One of his chief agents appears as a lamb. Step by step, every plan of his seems to have been patterned on something of God's.

Now it is true of course that imitation is the most dominant law of all life. It is one of the commonest laws governing all action, from childhood on. Originality does not mean an absence of imitation. It means unusual wisdom and judgment and insight in the selection, and combination into one's own action, of what is found in others. The basis is still imitation. The new thing called originality is the rare judgment in choosing what to imitate, and how to combine what is chosen. Yet mark that this great traitor-prince imitates slavishly what God has done. There is no trace of originality. His mental powers are second-class.

This is not so surprising as it may seem at first flush. He has cut himself off from God, the source of all life and wisdom. All life, physical and mental and of the spirit, is in God, and from Him. Satan has existence, but in breaking away from God he broke away from the source of wisdom, and of strong mental power.

The Immense Power of Experience.

Yet—yet, let it be very plainly underscored that he is far more than a match for you and

me.   That will be a bit humiliating to us, but
it is as true as it is humiliating.

Will you please notice why we are no match
for him here? First of all, because of his long
experience.   Will you mark that experience
counts for more in the practical action of life
than anything else.   For instance, a man with a
second-grade mind, or third-grade, but with a
long matured experience, will completely out-
class the man of first-rate mental powers who
has no experience.   Neither unusual matured
talent nor unusual advantages of University
schooling, unaccompanied by experience, can
hold its own for a moment in the action of life
against matured experience wisely applied.

Experience outclasses every other sort of
qualification, standing alone without the experience.   When you have been actually through
a difficult situation you have a grip and confidence for a similar situation that can be gotten
in no other way.   You are afraid of a strange
thing.   Ignorance breeds fear.   You have confidence about the thing you have done a thousand or a hundred times.   Experience brings
boldness.   It knows.

Satan has a very long experience.   It has
been maturing for thousands of years.   He
knows us men like we know the thing we know
best.   And in comparison with him in the matter of experience we men are the merest babes,

just drawing our first gasping breath. He has been at this thing for millenniums; we are just starting in. We are no match for this tempter, even though his mentality is second-rate.

And then there is a second reason why we are no match for him here. It is a humiliating reason too, but again as true as it is humiliating. It is this: our mentality is not first-class either, except as the Spirit of God sways our mental powers. The keenest, wisest brain is not first-class except as it lives in its own atmosphere, that is the breath of God. And as a matter of fact we, too, have cut ourselves off from our true atmosphere by sin. And even where we have come back into our native air, through the redeeming work of our Saviour and Lord, in so far as He is not allowed to dominate our mental powers we fall to second place. We have not the mental powers with which we were endowed. Now I think we would agree to the sad fact that compromise with evil and selfishness have become a law among those of us classed as Christian people. By common consent the Church of Christ is not swayed in the life of its members by that Jesus-Spirit of which we talked a while ago.

Unsurrendered Mental Powers.

Then there is even more to be said. There are a great many earnest, godly people, who are wholly surrendered in spirit and purpose to the Lord Jesus, but whose mental powers are not surrendered. These lie fallow. It almost seems sometimes as though mental stupidity, the blind unthinking following of religious leaders, is looked upon as a sign of unusual grace, instead of unusual stupidity.

When the Holy Spirit is allowed possession there follows a second mental birth, as well as a new spiritual birth. There is a new activity, a new mental life, a new keenness and strength of mental action. It is the Spirit's mode of action. And in so far as it is not our experience, the lack tells how far the Holy Spirit is *not* in control. It tells how far we have not surrendered our powers to His sweet life-giving sway. This is a second reason why we are no match for our spirit-foe who is ever close upon our heels. Full victory comes through the blood of the Lamb, and through our mental powers being actively swayed by the Spirit of God.

There are a few other traits that should be noted. Satan is a liar. His word cannot be trusted. He has rare skill in blending. He can mix truth and lie, fact and falsehood, so skilfully and cunningly that even the elect are de-

ceived. Only the constant knee-test can detect
some of his damnable blending; only eyes
habitually steeped in the light of the Word can
see the subtle tinging of false colours in his
fabrics.

All sorts of lies come from him, big lies and
small; white lies and black—the mean dirty-
white, gray-smoky-white kind seem to be a favourite. Social lies, business lies, personal lies,
Church lies, religious lies; lies that are lived and
acted; lies in the garments worn;—all sorts
come from him. He is fond of disguises, and is
skilled in the use of them. He hates the truth.

A Cowardly Weapon.

Then he is fond of using force. Violence
is peculiarly his weapon, from the stage of simply threatening to use it, on through its active
use both in personal and in large mass move-
ments. If one man kills another, it is commonly
called murder. If a big organized crowd of
men do the same thing in a more or less skilled
way, it is called war.

I am not discussing either the question of
armies or of warfare. That's a separate question, with many facts to be noted on both sides
before a fair conclusion can be reached. Many
of the great armies are simply huge policing or-
ganizations keeping order on the street where

the national crowds pass by, and jostle each
other in passing.

But violence, force, mere brute force is one
of Satan's favourite modes of action, and reveals his character. Settling differences by re-
sort to mere animal strength is of course putting the whole affair on the very lowest basis.
Mere might is made the standard of right,
though it almost always means putting the
wrong up as the right, or in place of it. All use
of this lowest means of attaining one's own
ends, whether among individuals or with crowds
of men, is from this great usurper-prince.

Its commonness in social life, using one's social advantage to crowd down, or crush another;
in business life, where it is so universally practised, using whatever advantage may come into
one's hands to crush a rival or compel him to
come to your terms; in political, and even in
Church circles, reveal how wide-spread is the
subtle influence of this great spirit-foe of ours.
It reveals, too, his personal characteristics.
There is nothing more contemptibly cowardly
than the use of mere force to attain one's ends.

This leads directly to another trait that should
be very sharply marked—Satan is a *coward*. He
is a mean, contemptible coward. He is fond of
bluster and brag. He will come with his suggestion of doubt to some dear old saint of God,
lying in a bed of illness, weak in body and tired

in mind, and will worry and tease and torment her until she is almost in despair. Ugh! he is a contemptible coward. He prefers to attack somebody weaker than himself.

He is afraid of our Lord Jesus. He has no courage for a stand-up, square fair fight with an equal. Under such circumstances he will slink off. He is afraid of us, too, when we cling so close to Jesus that we two are as one. Resist him, and he will sneak off, and hunt for some one off his guard. Now it is good to remember this trait of cowardice. Cling close to our blessed Master; never get out of His presence; resist this great coward in the great Name, and you are safe.

But with that put in this—he is *persistent*. He has bull-dog tenacity. He knows how to hang on. There is just one thing that will out-do his persistence, and that is our *insistence* in our Lord Jesus' Name. He can't stand that. When he hangs on you hang on just a bit longer. He is defeated, and he knows it. Our Lord is Victor, and we know that. The tempter's persistence is bluster. Steady insistence, steady claiming the power of our Lord Jesus' Name, insistence, steady insistence—he can't stand that.

At His Strongest—Weak.

A friend told me of her nephew, who was under her care for a time while his parents were in India. The family devotional reading was in the Book of Revelation. There had been some hesitation about taking up that book, when it came in regular order, lest the children might not understand. But with the aunt's insistence that the children could get more than one might think, it was decided to take it up. One day the little fellow abruptly said, " Satan will have two big punishments, won't he?" His aunt was surprised, and sought to draw out his thoughts. " He will be put into the pit and then into the lake of fire," the child said. Evidently he had taken in much more of the family reading than they had supposed. So his aunt tried to instruct him further. How well she succeeded is suggested by the little man's remark one night as he was going to bed. As though talking half to himself he said, " Satan is very strong, we can't do anything against him," in a tone that suggested an element of fear in his mind. Then his face brightened, and his tone of voice completely changed, as he said, " but with Jesus, we are a hundred times stronger." Then as he was being tucked in he said, " Oh, I should say with Jesus, we are a thousand times stronger."

That was wholesome reading and instruction

for that child. The two definite impressions of the greatness of the foe, and of the greater power of our Lord, and that that power was ours, will be of great value to him as he grows in his Christian life. We should couple our Master with ourselves as the boy did, " with Jesus, we are a thousand times stronger "—and more! Let's remember that. It will put new life into our insistence, and it will put our enemy to flight.

Satan tries to imitate the beauty and personal attractiveness which were his but have been spoiled by his sin. He has great power, he is a subtle organizer, and has a splendidly compacted organization of spirit-beings at his nod and beck. His mentality is distinctly of secondary grade, but his experience with us men is so long and matured and intimate that he has enormous advantage.

He has a devilish knack of tenacity, of persistence. He loves deceit and is peculiarly skilful in using it. Rugged honesty is one of the sure checkmates for shutting him up in a corner. He uses force and delights in its use. And he is a contemptible coward.

This reveals much of his supposed strength, much of his real strength, and reveals too, how much less is he than our wondrous Victor, the Lord Jesus. " Greater is He," so much greater that you can't put into words how much greater.

But you can *know* how much when the thick of the fight is on.

The intelligent surrender of all our powers and activities to the Mastery of our Lord, the thoughtful cultivation of the Holy Spirit's presence and practical sovereignty, the daily quiet time alone with God's Word, the spirit of humble dependence upon our Lord—these will bring to us a simple, sane sense in recognizing the enemy, regardless of disguises, and will make us strong in resisting and overcoming him at every turn of the road.

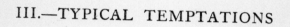

III.—TYPICAL TEMPTATIONS

EDEN: HOW THE TEMPTER WORKS

Three Attacks.

There have been three great attacks made upon man by the tempter, three great attempts to tempt him away from God's path—in Eden, in the Wilderness, and at Calvary. The purpose each time was the same—it was to swerve man from God's path and God's plan. That is the sole thing aimed at in each as in all temptation. In Eden man fell into the snare laid for him. He failed to obey God; he disobeyed. He obeyed another, and became the slave of him whom he obeyed. He lost his title to the dominion of the earth.

Our Lord Jesus came as the new Head of the race. He came to redeem what had been lost. His coming was a direct challenge to the traitor-prince. The challenge of His presence was met by the tempter in the Wilderness. It was the second great attack upon the race, the second temptation. That is, it was the second great driving attack.

Our Lord was tempted before the Wilderness. The Nazareth life was a continuation of temptations. And he was tempted by every sort of subtle and stormy effort during the three and a half years after. But the Wilderness was a great pitched battle. It was the first of two pitched battles. Our Lord remained true. He steadily insisted on obeying the Father. The tempter was defeated.

This led to the third great attack or attempt at Calvary. Having failed in the Wilderness, Satan would try again. He would make another yet greater effort. That second great effort was at Calvary. There he rallied all his power. This was the second great pitched battle of which our Lord was the central figure. And we men can never be grateful enough for the steadfast obedience, for the victory through obedience, of our Lord in the Wilderness, and at Calvary—for everything most dear to us was at stake. He was acting for us as our representative and substitute.

Calvary

The one thing aimed at by Satan at Calvary was to make obedience just as difficult and painful, and indeed as near to impossible, as it was possible for him to do. Obedience has never been so hard before nor since. By every bit of Satanic cunning and devilish malice of which he is such a consummate master, he hedged the path of obedience in. By thorns and thongs, club and cross, bodily pain, mental and spirit pain, by every conceivable indignity and shame and utter disgrace he sought to check Jesus'

advance, to choke Him back. It was Satan at *Calvary*
his very best, which means at his very worst.

The One Aim in Temptation.

But—blessed ever be the Name of Jesus—
He never flinched. He felt the pain, He felt
the shame. None ever realized and felt so
keenly all that was heaped upon Him. But He
obeyed. He despised the shame. We men can't
take in the depth of meaning of St. Paul's sentence, " becoming obedient, even unto death, *Phil.2:f*
yea, the death of the cross." [1] All the malice of
hell, all the devilish malignity and hatred of the
tempter, all the simple, steady obedience of
Jesus, our Lord, to the Father, all the matchless
love of the heart of God, are covered by that
little three-lettered " yea."

Here lies the core of all temptation, to make
us disobey, to ensnare us away from the Father's plan. Under every sort of device and
cunning this is the one thing being aimed at in
temptation. Through confusing our thoughts,
through blurring our conceptions of what is
right, through mixed standards of right and
wrong, through compromise of some sort, by
rush and grip of passion, by lure and glare of
ambition, by sudden sweep of storm, by sly
sneaking of the snake through the tall pretty

[1] Phil. ii. 8.

grass—under every sort of approach this is the one thing aimed at—to lead us to break, by little or by much, the Father's common plan for human life, or His particular plan for each life.

And here, too, lies the one simple pathway trodden by our Lord, obedience to the Father's plan, regardless of consequences. It is the pathway for us to tread, in the strength of our Lord's victory. His footprints are big and clear and sharply outlined. We are to place our feet where He trod. He has made the way easy. Keen ears to hear, clear eyes to see, under those a sturdy will to follow—then comes and stays the one simple standard of right, and yet better the grace and strength to stick to that standard; that is the unfailing road to victory over every temptation.

God has given us in His Word these great temptations, pictured out in clear outline, that we may know the wiles of the tempter and the wisdom of our Victor. We want to look a bit at two of these. Eden reveals how the tempter works. It should make us keener in watching. The Wilderness shows us how our Lord resisted him. It should make us keener in praying. Just now, a look at Eden.

The Eden Trail.

Eden was God's plan for man. Eden was
a garden. God planned a garden for our home.
There was perfect love, no questionings, no
doubtings, no suspicions, but the sweet, full
confidence of true perfect love. Love was the
atmosphere of the garden. That meant that
there was purity. True love always includes
sweet purity. There was no sin, no blemish, no
weakness, no wrong, but sweetest purity of
heart and life, of imagination and thought and
conduct.

And that in turn meant, too, that there was
companionship between God and man. Each
enjoyed the other. There could be fellowship
because there was perfect love, and the perfect
purity that belongs to love. There cannot be
fellowship between Him and us except upon His
level of purity and love. That rules us out
now utterly, except as we come back by the red-
dened pathway made for us by our Lord's death.
Through Him comes purity, and through Him
love is made perfect.

There is God's plan—a garden with its beauty
and fragrance, perfect love, perfect purity, full
fellowship between God and man, among men
themselves, and between man and the lower creation and all nature. That is the Eden plan,
God's plan for man.

Then, then the tempter came. Why did he come? Because he wanted to get control of this earth. That dominion had been given to man. He held his title by obedience. The tempter came to steal away man's control and usurp the earth. If man could be made to disobey by so much as a half of a hair's-width, the title would be defective, and the earth's dominion lost; the tempter would have mastery, not simply of the earth but of the man whose worship he coveted.

Will you mark very keenly *how* he came? Because that is the way he *comes*. We want to learn the Eden trail. It will help us become good trailsmen, good trail detectors. And that is an immense help. To recognize a temptation sharp and clear is one-half of the victory over it. We are studying the serpent trail here.

How he came.

Please note three points as to how he came. He came *under cover;* he used somebody else, or something else; he worked in disguise. That is immensely suggestive. Was he afraid to come out into the open? I think he was. Is he afraid? I have no doubt of it. Satan, coming plainly as he is, with the light we have, would be booted out most times, and with no easy booting either. And so he comes under cover.

It is his favourite way of working, under cover. He came through a serpent, through an animal. And mark you this, he got the very best he could; and he always does. The animal he used was the subtlest there was in the whole animal creation.

The word " subtlest " suggests this: not what it means to us sometimes—craftiness—not that; but mental keenness, if I may use the word " mental " for an animal. That is the thought of the word " subtle "—mental, intellectual keenness and acumen. He got the best there was, and behind that came his snaky, sneaky, crafty foot-tread; and he is still coming. He is the keen man who will find out how to detect Satan's disguises.

Then he made his attack *through the body;* and this again is immensely suggestive. The suggestion to Eve came through a perfectly natural bodily appetite, the desire for good food, something tasty and toothsome. Through that he came to her. And if you will mark very keenly again, it is one of his favourite modes. He came, and he comes through the body; through a purely natural, normal function of the body, the desire for food, the desire for drink. He still works through the natural functions of the body. You quickly think what they are, all in themselves perfectly right when held to their true uses.

And then having gotten into the body he comes through bodily weakness, through disarrangements of bodily functions. Through excess in the use of the body he can come in, and he does. And I think to-day he is having a very wide sway among men through his bodily approach, far more than we guess. And far more than we guess, too, there is deliverance from him in our bodies through our Victor, Jesus Christ.

Then he came *through the mind*. Indeed, he came to the mind to reach the body. Of course he spoke to Eve; he could not touch her body except through her consent. But he tempted and confused Eve mentally, got her ideas mixed up, put in false thoughts and wrong thoughts and wrong ideas, and half truths. He confused her mentally and so confused her morally, and so got the consent of her will to his own will. And I may say here just this, the whole thing he is driving at is to get the control of our will. But he cannot without our consent. Every man is a sovereign in his will. Every man stands alone in imperial solitude in the realm of his will. And so Satan tries to affect that, to control it.

He still works through our mind. He can cast on your mental vision disturbing, distorting, and startling thoughts. He does; and following that, he affects the whole mental life marvellously, far more than we suspect. I do not mean just now simply those who have been taken to insane asylums. Without doubt in large measure he is responsible for their condition, though always through their consent. Everything is through human consent. But the devil cannot use these folks very much. They have gone too far. He is far more concerned to influence mentally us folks who are reckoned to be sane. He is working upon our mental condition, seeking to confuse, and distort, and swing us away. Remember this, that just as there is far more victory in our bodies through Jesus Christ our Saviour than many of us know, so there is far more victory in the matter of clear minds, and quiet minds, and minds strong for the service of life, through the Lord Jesus Christ, on the ground of His blood, than we have guessed.

And so these are the three ways he came: under cover, through the body, through the mind.

The Generations of Doubt.

Then notice _what he did_. And please keep in your mind as we are talking, that we are tracing now the Eden trail. Wherever you find these things anywhere you are coming across the slimy trail of the serpent.

The first thing he did was to raise a doubt

about God's love. "Hath God said you shall not eat of any of the trees? What a hard God He is! Lovely trees! Delicious fruit! It was made to be eaten; it will nourish your body. What a cruel God He is! Can't you eat of this fruit? What an awful God you have got!" That is the suggestion, a doubt about God's love. And following the language of the book of Genesis I want to read to you the generations of this thing called doubt. There are ten tables of generations in the book of Genesis, and I am going to add one for our practical help just now.

Doubt! These are the generations of doubt, as Satan begat them that day. Satan begat doubt. It was doubt of God's love that was the first born. Doubt of God's love gave birth to doubt of God Himself. Doubt of God gave birth to doubt of everybody else. We are living in a world of doubt; we are suspicious of everybody; all the time watching others the wrong way; keeping a suspicious eye open. That is the second generation. And doubt always gives birth to misunderstanding. That is a large generation. There are a great many children born there. And misunderstanding gave birth to criticism; likewise a very large family, many of whom, most, or shall I say "all" of whom abide with us until this day. And criticism gave birth to hatred in all its various

forms; and the generations of hatred are violence in all its forms. And the children there
are, personally, murder; and on the wholesale,
war. These are the generations of doubt of
God's love which Satan begat that day in the
Garden of Eden. And a peculiar thing about
these generations of Satan is that they are so
long-lived. Methusaleh dies in infancy by
comparison.

The second thing that Satan did was to tell
a lie. Perhaps I need not stop long there. He,
of course, is called the father of lies, all kinds
of lies, if you will mark. There is quite a
large family here. I need hardly label them
all to-night. There are white lies and black
lies; there are small lies as men measure them,
and large lies; there are social lies and there
are business lies. There are lies that you live;
there are lip lies and life lies. The whole world
is filled with the lies that have grown out of
the first that Satan told; and they all come from
him. If you will mark very keenly again this
is a bit of the Eden trail. All lying by look
or lip or for any purpose, social, personal, religious—there is a large range of religious lies,
you know—the whole thing, the whole brood
can be traced directly to this great father of
lies.

The third thing—he kindled the fires of an
unholy ambition. And I would need to have

a whole evening for a talk on a thing of that kind. He gave to Adam and Eve an unholy ambition. He said to Eve, " Ye shall be as God! " Ah; there is Satan's ambition, to be as God! to be worshipped as God. He said to Eve, " You can by a simple act of your own lift yourself above this level where God has put you, to a level with God Himself." And all the wrong ambition of life had its birthplace and its birthtime there. I hardly know how to say briefly enough and simply enough what I want to say here. This itch seems very common everywhere. It is in commercial life; it is in social life, very, very strong; it is in political life; it is in business life; it is in church life; it is in every phase of life; the effort to get yourself up above where God has placed you by improper means. The feverish fingering of the door-knob upstairs, and the insistently working your way up the stairs where you have no right to be. The itch of an unholy ambition was the third thing he gave to Eve.

And the fourth was this, he urged disobedience. The one keyword of the true life is obedience. The keyword of Satan's life is disobedience to God. The one thing that our Lord Jesus Christ insisted on doing was this, obeying His Father. He could make bread, but He would not make it at Satan's suggestion. He waited until the Father said, " Feed those hungry " by Galilee's waters. The obeying the Father was the one touchstone of His life: and it must be the one touchstone of our lives.

> " More anxious not to serve Thee much,
> But please Thee perfectly."

But Satan that day introduced the further itch of disobedience.

And the fifth thing he tried to do; it came later, after the act of disobedience; please mark that very keenly; the fifth thing came *after* Eve gave him a very large door to get in, and it was this—a suggestion of impurity. The serpent does not speak of it: it comes as a mental suggestion. Mark keenly, in that third chapter there was no act of impurity, there is nothing wrong in the way of impurity except what is in the imagination of those two, which led to the seeking for garments, which were not intended in the first place for the body but wholly for the mind. And this is the commonest sin of the whole race, through all the world, from that day until this,—impurity, that is to say, if you will mark keenly again, simply this, the using of a perfectly proper, holy function in a way not intended. Simply that; but all of that. That is the core of impurity of every sort and shape and degree.

And I wish you would mark very keenly a

difference here in Satan's approach. Before their act of disobedience and afterwards his approach is different. Before that disobedience he came from the *outside;* afterwards he came from the *inside.* The serpent said, " Eat the fruit. God is not good!" But when the fruit was eaten the serpent was dismissed; his work was done. Through the act of disobedience there was an inner door open, and through that door the evil one came and put the image of the wrong thing on the mind. Before the eating he came from without; after the eating he came within. To-day, he comes both ways. He had only one way of coming in the beginning: now he has two, and he uses both.

Some of the Results.

Then I want you to notice, please, a fourth item in Satan's coming, *some of the results.* The first was this, voluntary separation by man from God. If you will mark again, please, the separation between God and man did not begin with God. It began with man. God did not go away; man went away. He hid himself behind a tree. That is a very bad use of trees. Trees were never meant for any such use as that of hiding away from God. And ever since man has been hiding from God. God does not go away; man does.

The second thing was this, and I wish you might mark this keenly if you will, a second result, moral cowardice. Notice what our splendid first man of the race said. " The *woman* Thou gavest me! *I* am not to blame; she is. What did You give me that woman for?" Blaming somebody else. Contemptible cowardice; but he does not stop there, " The woman *Thou* gavest; Thou art to blame after all; it is all Thy fault."

Moody tells about going to a prison in New York City and having a service, and then going down afterwards to talk with the prisoners one by one, and he said, " I never found such an innocent lot of men in my whole life as in that place. Each man explained that somebody else was to blame." Adam seems to have given birth to a great race of moral cowards. " *I* am all right. It is *her* fault! It is *his* fault. Watch *him!* Look back *here!* Keep an eye on that man, I am all right!" Moral Cowards. They are extremely common.

And then a third result I wish you might mark yet more keenly was this—fear. Sin always produces fear, and I wish I had time this evening to talk about this, the fears that affect body and mind. If I could remove from your minds all sense of fear to-night you would go out of this hall made over new in your bodies as well as in your mental power. Fear is one

of the most slavish results of sin. Adam said,
" I was afraid, I was afraid." And he repeated
the sentence that is used more times on human
lips than any other, I think. " I am afraid! I
am afraid! I am afraid." It is so common that
we use it when we are not afraid. But the
sense of fear is woven into the whole life of
the race. And fear always affects the body,
intensely and potently and subtly. If I am
swayed by a spirit of love and a perfect confidence my body is freer; its functions are dis-
charged more freely; I am stronger physically;
and I am clearer mentally. But fear locks up
the body. It deprives it of its strength; it affects the mind; it affects the whole nature,
body, mind, and spirit. The whole thing began
that Eden day.

Now that is the Eden trail. Have you ever
seen it down your way? Is it a strange trail to
you? If you have seen it, or any part of it,
you may know it is by that old Satan serpent.
You don't see him; he is under cover; but you
see his trail. It is very plain in the Bible. If
you will run through the whole Book of God,
you see the serpent trail. Satan himself is
mentioned only a very few times. I can almost
repeat the times, they are so few. But his trail
is everywhere.

What about the trail in the Book of life?
Any trail down your way? Shall I repeat these

things? Doubt, with its offspring of misunderstanding, criticism, and violence; lying, unholy ambition, disobedience, impurity, moral cowardice, fear, bodily disorder, mental disorder, the lack of a clear, quiet, sane mind! How about the trail? Because wherever that trail is, in small degree or large, there is evidence of the serpent's presence.

And coming to the close of our quiet talk together, and I wish you might listen very quietly here, if there be any of this sort of thing, any doubt of God, any failure to obey, any moral cowardice, lies of any colour or any size or degree, any sense of fear which means a lack of a quiet faith, any using of a pure holy bodily function in a way not intended, if there be any of these, then you may know that there, hidden away, maybe half out of sight, but allowed his corner, is *Satan*.

I wonder how many of us are giving the enemy covert and comfort. I suggest that we go into some quiet corner, and breathe the prayer of the Psalmist, " Search me, oh God, and know my heart, and help me know what Thou dost know; try me, and know my thoughts, motives, purposes, loves, innermost, undermost; and help me know what Thou dost know. And lead me to see if there be any way in me that grieves Thee and gives Satan a hold against Thee." And then, if you will, add this bit to your prayer,—" Lead me *out* of that way, into *Thy* way, the way everlasting."

And if perchance you are thinking, " Ah! you don't know how tight on my life some of these things are; you don't know how fear can grip, and disobedience grip, and cowardice grip, and other unnamed things, how they can grip." And you say, " How can I put them out? " Well, the last word just now is this, the last word is from the last book of the Bible. Our message was from the beginning of the first book. The last word is near the last of the last book,[1] " They overcame him because of the blood of the Lamb." That is the common reading. But I like the other reading of it: " They overcame him on the ground of the Blood of the Lamb."

I want to tell you this—there is only liberty to-night from every bit of the Eden trail through the Blood of the Lamb; only so; but so. Bodily disorder, bodily weakness, mental disturbance, fear, impurity, doubt, disobedience, moral cowardice, lies, all the rest of it; there is victory over all through the Blood of our Lord Jesus Christ. And while we have been thinking of that precious blood as the entrance into the Christian life, let us remember this, that day by day there is victory for us, and there is freedom for us from every bit of the whole Eden trail, on the ground of the Blood of our

[1] Revelation xii. 11.

Lord Jesus Christ, the Lamb of God. Shall we
go out to-night and see to it that Satan is
undercut so far as we are concerned, and that
the Lord Jesus Christ may have the use of us
as He will in His great outreaching plan for
His world?

THE WILDERNESS: HOW THE TEMPTER IS DEFEATED

Forestalling the Tempter.

We have talked a bit about the temptation by Satan, in Eden, upon Adam, the first head of the race. Now we want to talk about the second great attack by Satan upon our race, through its second Head, our Lord Jesus Christ. And I want first of all to remind you of this, that the temptation in the Wilderness was a necessity. It was a necessity for Satan because his kingdom was in peril, and he must fight for that which he wanted. It was a necessity for our Lord Jesus Christ as the new Head of our race, because He was to worst the tempter in the temptation, and win back the dominion of the whole earth for our human kind.

I think we will, perhaps, understand a bit better the necessity of the Wilderness temptation if we remember this, that when Adam was created he was given the dominion over the earth; he was the earth's undermaster. He was lord of the creation by the Father's appointment. The prince of darkness was eager to get that dominion for himself from man and over man, and through man, and so he made the attack in Eden, and man fell and Satan succeeded.

Now our Lord Jesus Christ stepped on the scene to win the earth, and the whole race of men, back to its original allegiance to His Father. Satan must fight Him. Satan was stealing men's allegiance by deceiving them. The temptation in the Wilderness was a necessity for Satan because he must fight his way against the new Man, God's new Man. His stolen kingdom was in peril because of this Lord Jesus. The Wilderness temptation was a necessity to Jesus Christ because in it He met the head of the opposing forces and foiled him. The victory of Calvary has the first striking of its note in this temptation. In winning over Satan there He began His victory on Calvary. And, if you mark it keenly, the whole kingdom of evil spirits knew of the Lord Jesus' victory in the Wilderness. Whenever and wherever He came they were afraid and fled.

I want to say what I have to say under three very simple heads. The *first,* the Holy Spirit's preparation for the temptation. I ask you to mark the fact that the Holy Spirit made preparation for this temptation. He took control of the situation. The initiative in this temptation was not taken by Satan; it was taken by the

Holy Spirit. It says very plainly, "Then was Jesus led up by the Spirit into the wilderness to be tempted!"[1] He took the initiative. He displayed masterly generalship. He did not wait until the tempter came, but obliged the tempter to come. He forced the fighting. It was a fine bit of generalship. We ought to follow His lead far more there. Most of us, may I say, wait until we are tempted, and then, half-scared, seek for help. But we should always pray ahead, and watch ahead, and take the ground before the Evil One can come. That is what the wondrous Holy Spirit does here. He forestalled the evil one.

At one time Mr. Moody was on an ocean liner, in a great storm, and they were sure the boat was going to the bottom. They were all praying; everybody prays in a bad storm, you know. A gentleman told about going to one of the decks, and to his great surprise he saw Mr. Moody standing on the deck, not in the prayer meeting down below, but standing quietly looking out over the raging waters. And he said, "Why! Mr. Moody, aren't you down in the prayer meeting?" And in his quiet way Mr. Moody said, "Oh! I am prayed up."

There is a marvellous generalship in praying ahead. We must not wait till we are driven to pray, if we would forestall the evil one. Do

[1] Matthew iv. 1.

as the Holy Spirit does here. He took charge
of the situation. That is the first suggestion in
the Holy Spirit's preparation.

The Holy Spirit's Generalship.

And then the second suggestion is this. He
took possession of our Lord Jesus. Jesus was
filled with the Holy Spirit. The Holy Spirit
took possession of our Lord. Before the temptation came, the Spirit filled Him with Himself,
to meet the temptation.

And yet I want to remind you of this, and I
ask you to listen keenly that you may not misunderstand—the Lord Jesus was not filled with
the Holy Spirit in a sense peculiar to Himself.
Now I say that reverently, but I say it because
of this,—He insisted at every point in living
the life of a man, dependent entirely upon the
Holy Spirit. And the thing to mark is this,
that just as the Son of Man as man was filled
by the Holy Spirit before the temptation came,
that He might meet and resist the temptation,
even so you and I will be filled if He may have
His way, filled beforehand that we may meet
temptation as He did, prepared ahead. It is
immensely suggestive to us. So many of us
play a back-handed game. We wait until we
are pushed, and then we do the best we can.
If we yield to the Holy Spirit's sway we will

be prepared ahead and force the fighting, and make the devil hunt his corner.

Then note very keenly, please, the Holy Spirit took charge of our Lord's temptation; not in a peculiar way; in just the same way that He takes supervision of our temptation. He takes supervision of all our temptations. The whole thing is to yield to His filling, to His sway; He takes care of the rest. In 1 Corinthians x. 13 we are told, " There hath no temptation taken you but such as man can bear: but God . . . will not suffer you to be tempted above that ye are able." He is the Superintendent of our temptations. If we yield to His sway, he attends to the victory always. If we appreciated this, it would change our whole attitude toward temptation.

Most folks fear temptation. We are afraid of it. We are afraid we will be tempted. But instead of that we ought to think of the temptation as a chance to defeat the devil. A temptation is two things: it is a chance to make the devil go; secondly it is a chance to win a great victory. We ought not to think of the temptation from the evil one's side only, who will overcome us if we stand alone. Were we to magnify the Holy Spirit, and think of the temptation from *His* side, that would mean a fresh defeat for the tempter, and a fresh consciousness of the victory of our Lord Jesus Christ. We

would go to the ground of the temptation, in
the path of duty, never otherwise, but we would
go there with a zest because we know in our
Lord's power it means victory, and it means defeat; defeat for Satan, and the victory of our
Lord Jesus anew in our lives.

Then please mark keenly, the Holy Spirit
stays with our Lord Jesus through the temptation. He took charge ahead of the whole situation; He prepared our Lord for the temptation
as a man; He stayed with Him throughout.
There is one thing you can count on all the time,
the blessed Holy Spirit's presence with us. He
does not leave us. If there is any parting of
company here, it must be after the old Eden
pattern; that is, *you* go, God doesn't go. It
was Adam who hunted the cover of the trees.
The blessed Holy Spirit stays.

And then the fourth thing to mark in the
Spirit's preparation is a very keen thing, the
place of the temptation. The place was the
Wilderness. The Wilderness of Judea practically begins at the door, or the gate of Jerusalem, and it runs down that eastern slope to the
great Dead Sea. What does the Wilderness mean?
What does the Dead Sea mean? You know. It
is the greatest sin-scar on the surface of the
whole earth. There were the cities of the plain,
beautiful and fruitful as Eden, as the garden of
the Lord for beauty and fertility. They are

sunken out; they are swept away. Judgment upon sin is scarred into the earth's surface. Will you mark keenly that the Dead Sea—and the Wilderness is the fringe of the Dead Sea—the Dead Sea, the whole Wilderness is the fact of judgment upon sin scarred into the very earth's surface. If folks do not believe the Bible, the Old Testament, let them go to the Dead Sea, and simply study the case historically. The Dead Sea speaks out the terrible fact of sin, and the sure coming of judgment upon sin.

Now this is the place where the temptation took place. Who chose it? Satan? Not a bit of it. It was the last place he would choose. He did not like the Wilderness. It was too uncomfortably familiar to him; it told too much of his trail for him to choose it. No! The Holy Spirit set the first bit of the temptation in the place where sin's scar was burned deepest in. A bit of his strategic generalship!

And then, fifth point in this preparation of the Holy Spirit, the *time* of the temptation, forty days. That is to say a long time. It was a full test; it was a severe test. You know the time test is the hardest test. We are all fairly good, I suppose, at short-suffering, but a few of us do not know much about long-suffering. "The fruit of the Spirit is . . . long-suffer-ing." [1]   The time test is the hardest test for

[1] Galatians v. 22

everybody. You keep sweet for a while, but how about keeping sweet all the while. Forty days long the Holy Spirit plans the temptation for Satan. Listen, keenly, that Satan may have the fullest sweep of his power, and do his best and his worst, and that he might know a certain defeat, and the more certain because the temptation lasted so long.

And just one last minor suggestion under that preparation is this—the wild beasts were there. What does that suggest? Would they help the Lord, do you think? Or would they hinder? That bit about the wild beasts is an added touch to show the terribleness of the situation for the man Jesus. I wish I had a company of missionaries here just now, foreign missionaries, to remind them particularly, and all of us, that a calm confidence in our Father gives us peculiar power over the whole lower creation. Man was given the dominion over the lower creation, and as we rest in the victory of our new Head, the Lord Jesus, we shall just quietly, calmly, meet any situation, any wild beasts. A calm confidence in the Father gives man his real dominion power over the lower creation.

Our Lord's Unfailing Response.

The second point that I want to speak of is our Lord's response to the temptation. He was

"in the Spirit." That means this, He yielded
the control of His life to the Holy Spirit. That
is the first "how" of meeting temptation, a surrender, complete, unfaltering, habitual, to the
sovereignty, the gracious mastery of the Holy
Spirit. That is the first bit in His response.
He was "in the Spirit," yielding to the mastery
of the Holy Spirit.

And the second bit here is this: full simple
obedience to the Father. You search through
these records in Matthew and Mark and Luke,
and mark the emphasis more and more on this,
that our Master's strength in all His temptation,
as in all His life on its purely human side, was
this, His full, simple, cheery obedience to His
Father's will, because it was His Father's will.
I would say, not because it appealed to His
judgment, but because it was His Father's will.
Doubtless it did appeal to His judgment, but if
our Lord had been obliged to obey the Father
where He did not understand why He should,
He would have obeyed blindly.

That is the very key on the human side to
His whole marvellous career from Nazareth on
to Calvary. There was an acquiescence in the
Father's plan because it was the Father's plan,
and there was a confidence in the Father's love.
He knew He could trust His Father. This is
the very underneath basis of His side of this
whole story. I may open my Bible to the first

chapter of the first page of Genesis, and if I were to read every passage or illustration of obedience or failure to obey I must stop at every page clear through. Obey! obey! obey! simply, intelligently, the will of the Father, because it is the Father's will, whether you see your way out or not. That is the very underground work of our Master's victory in the wilderness.

And then the third bit is this. He used the Word of God. I suppose it is true that men have superstitiously worshipped the old Book of God, merely as a book. And yet, keeping that in mind as a thing to be avoided, the use of the Word of God cannot be over magnified. It is God's own Word. There is more than print here. There is a Person here, in these very pages, speaking to us of our need and our hearts. Our Lord Jesus used the Word of God in meeting the adversary. And we shall see by and by what the adversary thought of that method.

The Temptation itself.

Then mark the temptation itself. The temptation ran through forty days. The bit we get is simply the climax. Those three great temptations are simply the last terrific onset, but the temptation has run through forty days, as

Mark's note makes quite clear. And you can imagine how subtle old Satan was. How suavely and sneakily and smoothly the old serpent began his attack. Through forty days it ran until the climax in the bit that is given to us.

It was a real temptation. Our Lord was tempted. That is to say, please listen keenly, and do not misunderstand, it could not have been a temptation unless there was present the possibility of a yielding to temptation. There is no temptation where there is no possibility of yielding to it. You can say on one side of the question that our Lord could not yield. Theoretically, ethically you say quite truly, that He could not yield to temptation. But practically it was entirely possible for Him to yield. He was really tempted. He faced the question of yielding. He felt the power of each temptation. But He asserted His will, and in full dependence upon the blessed Holy Spirit, He met the tempter at every point. He did not meet the temptations as Son of God; please remember that. When you are tempted, please remember that He met every temptation as a *man,* just as we must meet ours, and as we may meet them in dependence upon the Holy Spirit.

The first temptation was an appeal to the body. Just as in Eden so still he tempts through the body. It is a favourite mode. Satan is still coming to each of us through our bodies, far more than we suspect. The temptation was to a perfectly proper appetite. The desire for food is a perfectly normal desire. Satan prefers the normal paths of life. He always comes along the regular road of life. And then he approached Him at His likeliest point. The likeliest point, the openest point was the hunger, a perfectly normal condition of His body. He is always watching for the likeliest point. And because a man's strong point is very apt to become, in turn, his weak point, therefore guard your strong points and guard your weak points, and, I would suggest, guard all between, from my experience.

Then note the temptation itself: Satan said, "If Thou be the Son of God." I think the better reading in English would be this, "Since Thou art"; "If" in the sense of "since." "If" raises a doubt about Jesus Christ's divinity, and asks Him to *prove* it. "Since" means he is asking our Lord to *use* His divinity to help out His humanity. It was a temptation not to *prove* that He was divine, but to *use* divine power to help Himself as a man. Jesus said, "Man shall not live by bread alone." Satan said, "You are Son of God; go up to the God level." "Ah, no," our Lord says, "I came down for my brothers' sake. I will never leave My brothers. I will stay with My brothers. I will meet every temptation as My brothers must meet it. *Man* shall not live by bread alone, but by every word that proceedeth out of the mouth of God."

He answered as a man. I love that. Our Lord was a man, tempted in all points like as we are. He knows how things are going with you : He knows all about your life. He comes down alongside in the Wilderness and says, " Let us pull together. I will stay right by you."

The second bit in the answer was this, *full trust*. He said, " Even if I starve, My Father will attend to that. Maybe I will starve. I have had nothing for forty days, nothing but stones. You can't live on stones. It looks like starving. Well, I am willing to starve if that is the Father's wish. I am not concerned ; the Father will take care of the starving. Man shall not live by bread alone, but by every word of God." And this is far more true to-day in the things that touch our physical strength than most of us know yet.

The thing that Satan asked Him to do was not wrong in itself. Our Lord supplied food afterwards in far greater measure. The mere changing of stones to loaves would not have been wrong, if underneath the Father was guiding. But the wrong would have been in doing anything that the evil one suggested. And I want to say this, it is bad to do good at Satan's suggestion. It is a very common thing among Christian workers to say " This is a good thing to do." Yes, this is a good thing to do— *if* the Master told you to do it. It is not good to do good unless it is God's will for you.

Now mark very keenly the effect upon Satan. He left that temptation. Practically he gave in. He could do nothing. Apparently he closed. If you notice keenly you will see he closes only to start again. Have you found that out? If you have met him at one point of temptation, and he has left you, just remember this, he is around the corner figuring out where he can best strike in next. He leaves to come back. The Word of God forces him to leave. It is very striking: he is afraid of that Book. The quotation shuts him up at once. He leaves, yet only to shift the attack, only to come back on another line of approach.

" Lead us not into Temptation."

The second temptation cunningly plays upon our Lord's mood. Our Lord says, " Not by bread, but by trust." " Ah! " the devil says, " we will just play on His trust in His Father. He is in a deeply religious mood. We will have a religious temptation." And so he shifts the scene. I think he is very glad to do this. He gets away from that Wilderness; he is uncomfortable there. He takes the very height of the temple. It is a religious atmosphere. I sometimes think the temptations hardest to meet are those that have a religious setting.

The tempter said this time, " Since Thou art God's Son, cast Thyself down." That is to say, " You trust the Father. That is splendid! Now just show the world how you do trust Him. Cast yourself down before it, and they will accept you as their Messiah. Just show all the world how you trust your Father." Satan preaching the Gospel of Trust! Have you ever known that temptation? I have.

There is an inner response here. The inner response to the first temptation is in the hunger; the inner response here was His settled purpose to trust His Father. But His reply comes, " Thou shalt not test. To throw Myself down would be testing God's love. Does God love? I will not test it. I will rest upon it. Love never tests. Love trusts. Thou shalt not make test of the Lord thy God, but go in the way He leads."

The third temptation was the last attempt. Satan takes Him up to a high mountain and shows Him the whole world, the glory of it, with a very quick panoramic view. It is not an impossible thing to do in that country, for Moses from one of those neighbouring mountain tops saw the whole land. So Satan comes to Him with a swift world view. He thought he would sweep the Master off His feet. Again this is one of his favourite methods.

A great many people have met the first temptation and resisted; and the second and resisted; and have been swept off their feet by the dazzling view of the third. I think it is pathetic to the point of weeping to find how one leader after another in Christian service has been swept off his feet by a dazzling view of the kingdom of this world, and been set aside as no longer useable by the Father. It was the temptation of the Church in Constantine's time, and some of us think the Church has never recovered from that temptation of the fourth century.

There is a real temptation here, an inner response. Man was given the dominion of all the world; that belongs to us. And our Lord Jesus was come down to restore that dominion. Here is the point of inner response. Somebody might say, " Did Satan really think that the Lord Jesus Christ would do such a thing as fall down and worship him? " At first flash you might say, " No, surely he could not think that." But the more you think into it, the more you see that his proposition is this: " Let us make a combination. You tie up with me. Of course God is over all, and you will have the dominion of the world, which is your right. Let us combine." It is a favourite word of his—" combination." It has slipped many a man off his feet who has given in a bit to the devil, working under cover, that he might have the dominion over the kingdom. I sometimes think it has led more, far more, Christian leaders off their feet than have been able to withstand its dazzling lure.

The answer was, " Get thee hence." That is a bit that I like. " Leave ! " Don't ask him to go; *tell* him to go. And the marvellous thing is this, he obeyed.

And just one word as we close our talk together. What did our Lord Jesus mean in the prayer He gave us to use when He taught us to say, " Lead us not into temptation "? It has puzzled a good many to know just what that means. Would God lead a man into temptation? What does that mean? There are three or four interpretations, and each have some shade of truth. But I keep swinging back to this: this is what the Master meant, " *You* cannot stand being tempted alone. You alone cannot stand temptation. I know; I have been there; I have been there forty days. I know temptation as no other man knows it, in its storm, in its subtlety, in its persistence." And now He says, " The thing for *you* to do is this. I have gotten the victory. You pray, ' Lead *me* not into temptation, but help me in fighting, help me to live *under the shadow of Thy victory.*' "

You cannot meet temptation alone. You are no match for the evil one. There is not one of us here who is any match for him. It is only as we come up close to our Lord Jesus, under the shadow of His Cross, that we get victory. But we can get it there. Let us remember that Revelation word,[1] "They overcame him on the ground of the Blood of the Lamb, *and* the word of their testimony" carried to the point of a sacrificial life. May our Lord Jesus Christ help us to live in the strength of *His* victory.

[1] Revelation xii. 11.

IV.—THE SECRET OF VICTORY

IN THE VICTOR

The Tempter afraid of Jesus.

Fear is the beginning of defeat. I do not mean the fear of reverence, but fear that is afraid. Of course defeat is a fighting word. It means that the enemy has been recognized and resisted. There are persons who do not know fear because they don't recognize the enemy, and don't oppose him. They move smoothly along the lines of least resistance regardless of moral issues. The absence of a sense of fear there simply tells of cowardice and childishness. But where the fight is on, and blows being exchanged, there fear is a sure element of defeat.

It recognizes and realizes that some one greater and stronger is actively opposing, and that makes it shrink and tremble. A false fear *thinks* the enemy is stronger. Real fear knows it. Fear sucks the spirit out of one's fighting, it takes the nerve out of one's courage, and the vim and zest out of one's action. Fear is the beginning of defeat.

Now the tempter knows fear. That is a fact of great comfort for us. And the fear he knows is not a false one; it is founded on fact and experience.   He has met One greater and stronger than himself.   The two have measured strength in a long and bitterly waged contest. And he knows the bitter sting of defeat.   That defeat taught him fear.   He is afraid of his Victor.   He knows what it means to be thwarted and resisted, beaten back steadily, and defeated clear off the fighting ground.   There has been a man upon the earth of whom Satan is afraid, whom he can neither touch nor resist—that man is Christ Jesus.

Satan is afraid of our Lord Jesus.   He learned to fear Him in Nazareth early in the fight.   In the Wilderness fear became a real force in his life, weakening, dispiriting, and even terrifying him.   That Wilderness siege of temptation was as carefully planned out as it could be.   It began on Satan's part with eagerness mingled with fear.   There was eagerness because everything the tempter prized and wanted was at stake. There was fear because of his previous dealings with our Master during those Nazareth years.   Though the Wilderness temptation began with eagerness and fear, it ended with rage and a fearsome terror, because this new Man, Jesus, was so strongly steady in His obedience to the Father.   Satan was having a new experience.   There was something new and strange and terrifying to him in this quiet, steady, obedient Man, who knew only Another's plan for

His life. The tempter became afraid of Jesus, and is afraid of Him.

The Tempter couldn't touch Jesus.

The tempter could not touch Jesus. He tempted Him at every turn, but he could make no impression. His sword only dulled and nicked and bent against the rock of Jesus' steady obedience. He attacked in every conceivable way, and at every possible opening, but his attacks failed. The person of our Lord was the bright centre attracting the keenest shafts the enemy could hurl. But His person never was touched until the hour came when Jesus chose to yield. The Nazareth precipice, the Jerusalem stones, the storm on Galilee's blue waters whose unusual violence frightened those old storm-beaten sailors—each in turn failed to *touch* the person of Jesus. There was absolutely no way of getting *within* to attack. And all outer attacks failed until Jesus chose—for a great purpose, as counselled and foreknown [1] by the Father—to yield up His person and His life. The tempter could not touch Him, and failed in every attempt.

And more striking yet, the tempter could not resist Jesus. Jesus did not act on the defensive merely. He was aggressive. He attacked Sa-

[1] Acts ii. 23.

tan. His very presence here was a challenge and an attack. Every demon cast out, every disease healed, every advancing step on His onward way, every hour spent in public ministry, every personal interview with a cultured Nicodemus, or a Sychar outcast, was an attack on the enemy's stronghold. Each bit of steady, faithful obedience to the Father, each touch of gentle love upon human life, each warm, sympathetic approach to needy men, each humble, self-forgetful giving of Himself out in glad service for others—each was an aggressive attack upon the " strong man," whom He had come to rout out of his usurped territory.

And the tempter could not resist these attacks. He was defeated at every turn. Satan is afraid of Jesus our Lord. And well he may be. There has been a man down on the earth of whom Satan was afraid, whom no attack of his could touch, and whose attacks in turn he could not resist, try as he would.

Why was the tempter afraid of Jesus? Why is he afraid of Him? Aside from this experience with our Lord, he has not been in the habit of showing fear. The general impression he has given has been one of boldness, of a daring, fearless driving on. What is the explanation of this fear? Why was our Lord Jesus able to resist his temptations and attacks so unfailingly, and then to completely turn the tables and make this great spirit-being actually flee, terror-stricken, before His attacks?

It seems almost like a useless question, because the great strength of our divine Victor, and the sweeping character of His victory have been so acknowledged and embalmed in the hymns and literature of the Church. Yet there is no question better worth asking just here. For the answer will make us sing the praises of our wondrous Jesus-Saviour with all the more fervour of heart. And it will do more than that, too. It shows us the path of victory along which we must walk if we would know the power of His victory in our daily lives.

No Sin.

There are five things to be noted in the answer. Two of them are negative things, but of immeasurable positiveness in their very negativeness. The other things are positive in form as well as in fact.

The first thing to note is this: there was no sin in Jesus. It tried to get in. Most careful search was made for any crevice or crack of an opening however slight, through which sin could find an entrance. But no entrance was ever found. He was sinless. He Himself challenged His foes to find any sin in Him.[1] That

[1] John viii. 46.

was a daring thing to do. It was the daring of
purity and of truth. Certainly if there had been
sin or fault these were the very men to have
found it, and ruthlessly held it up to the strongest light. By consent of all who had to do with
Him during the hours of His trial and death, He
was free from sin so far as could be discerned.
The agreement among doubters and critical
sceptics regarding the perfection of His character is most striking.

I am speaking wholly now of the practical
side of this fact. Leaving aside all discussion
just now of the nature of our Lord's person,
and of the theoretical possibility of His sinning
—this is the bit of truth which I want to emphasize now : Jesus was sinless because He chose
to be. He refused to sin. He resisted earnestly
and actively and prayerfully every temptation to
sin.

Practically sin is entirely a matter of the will.
It is an act of choosing. Our Lord chose to
keep sin out. He had the immense advantage of
having no inheritance of sin to weaken Him.
Against the most cunning and insidious attempts,
He deliberately and habitually chose not to sin.
It cost Him effort. It meant active choosing on
His part, a constant choosing. It meant as great
a use of will power as ever human made. He
was obliged to choose. All about Him, the presence of sin and temptation forced Him to

choose. His sinlessness practically consisted in this, that He chose not to sin.

A New Experience for the Tempter.

This was something new to the tempter, strangely new. It was perplexing and non-plussing. He had had no such experience all through his long career of tempting. Only once had he met a couple who had no sin inheritance to trouble them. And by a bit of cunning they had been deceived and were quickly ensnared. That was long, long before. This man with His steady purpose to please the Father, this Jesus was utterly disconcerting. The tempter could do nothing against such a man.

This sinlessness, both in will and in act, in purpose and in life, was the basis of our Lord's victory. It was the basis of Satan's defeat. He feared such a Man. He could not touch Him. He could not resist Him. It was this that gave and gives such value to Jesus' death on our behalf. It was a sinless life that was poured out to the very death on Calvary. This very fact made His death *wholly* on account of others. Of Himself Jesus would never have died. For death is the logical outcome of sin. Where there is no sin, either by entail or act, there is no death. The purity and obedience, the perfection and sinlessness of the Man who died, gave the great value to that death. Of very necessity it was for others. Here is the ground-work of the stinging defeat administered to the tempter by our Lord.

It was the sinlessness of this Man who gave up His life that made His death such a satis-fying forever of the righteousness of God. It was the utter lack of all claim upon Jesus by Satan, that made His death settle forever so utterly all of Satan's claim against us sinners. Herein was shown the wondrous love that melts the stubbornness of the human heart into peni-tent softness. Jesus need not have suffered and died as He did unless He chose to. But He made that choice for our sakes. It was His love that led Him to that choice. This deliberate, determined keeping of sin out was the basis of the tempter's defeat.

Sin is Satan's doorway into a human life. Wherever there is sin there is a wide open door to him. Where there is no sin, as with our Lord, there is no opportunity of getting in. Sin is Satan's only doorway in. Sin is Satan's stronghold. It gives him footing for his fight-ing. It gives him atmosphere. No sin means no chance for Satan to work. Absence of sin cuts the very ground out from under his feet. I am talking about our Lord's sinlessness just now. But we shall see a little later the prac-tical power of this tremendous fact in our own lives. In this refusing to let sin in Jesus was utterly neutralizing Satan's power.

No Self.

The second thing in Satan's defeat by our Lord is this: there was no self-seeking in Jesus. That is included, of course, in saying that there was no sin; for sin at its core is self-seeking, that is, preferring one's own way to God's. Now Jesus was wholly unselfish; there was none of the self-spirit in Him.

We ought to take a moment to talk of just what that means. It does not mean a carelessness or a thoughtlessness about the needs of His bodily life. It is not selfish to care properly for one's health and strength, in the matters of food and sleep, air and exercise, and needful dress. One can easily go to a selfish excess in these things, and that is very common. That temptation is always at hand. And one can go to the other extreme of not giving thought and care enough to these things.

And if you will note it, this is just as selfish as the other extreme, though it is a sort of thoughtless, unconscious, unintentional selfishness. It is selfish because it is very sure to lead to conditions that will make one a charge upon or a care to somebody else. And at the same time we are not able to do for others what they need. Whatever makes one weaker in any way, which by due care and thought could have been avoided, has the taint of selfishness at its root.

Our Lord's unselfishness, undoubtedly, would be the genuine, thoughtful sort that made Him take proper care of His bodily needs and strength for other's sake, as well as because it was right in itself. And in this He gives an example that many earnest godly people need to take note of and follow.

And His lack of the self-spirit does not mean the ignoring of His personal identity, or of the great service entrusted to Him. He continually asserted His personal identity, telling plainly who He was, and why He had come, and that He was sent by the Father for a great mission among men.

What is Unselfishness?

His unselfishness meant simply this, that He lived for the Father, and for others, not for Himself. The passion of His life was for His Father. Selfishness at its core means that the passion is for one's self. The passion of Satan's heart is wholly and only for himself. Unselfishness is the strong thoughtful giving of one's self out in doing the Father's will in glad service among men.

Selfishness is a passion for self; unselfishness, or selflessness, is a passion for God, and that always means for others in their need. The streams of life naturally turn out. Wherever Satan has been able to control or influence with His subtle cunning, those streams all turn in. And wherever the streams all turn in there is a Dead Sea. Many a man's life, many a so-called Christian man's life, is simply the coast-line of a Dead Sea. We ought to be studying more carefully the direction of the current of that stream, I mean the under-current.

Jesus was swept by a passion for Another. He was utterly unselfish, selfless in this strong, good meaning. And, if you will please note very sharply, He was so because He chose to be. The air about Him was thick with temptations luring the other way. He had to choose, and, very reverently let me say, that that choice was not easy. It took a real, positive, continual action by His will.

The self-life came to Jesus in very subtle guise. The temptation to self-assertion for His own sake came to Him incessantly throughout that humble Nazareth life clear up to the tragic end of Calvary's ninth hour. But neither self-pity nor misunderstandings of His purpose by others, nor the pleadings of mistaken love, as when His mother seems to have sought—not realizing what she did—to use her influence with

Him, none of these swerved Him. He chose to keep all considerations of self severely out.

In this He was simply being true to the decision that sin should find no entrance. And in this He was defeating Satan. Self-seeking is the inner heart of the Satan-spirit. It gives him footing and freedom. The absence of the self-seeking spirit was a complete under-cutting of Satan. In that He emphasized His own victory, and Satan's defeat. Every advancing hour of His life made greater that victory, and that defeat, until the great climax at Calvary.

These are the two tremendous negatives in Jesus' human character that underlie the great victory. And no words could ever tell how much of strong choosing power was called forth by these two negatives—no *sin,* no *self.*

Obedience.

Then there are three positive traits underlying that defeat and victory. The first of these is obedience. Jesus was obedient. I have already spoken of this, and emphasized it. It cannot be spoken of too often, or two much. It is a truth practically lost by the Church that obedience is the first law of the true life. There has been much service, but little obedience, proportionately.

There may be much of self, of pride, of mere

human energy in service, and there is. Obedience may be humiliating, and painful; quite likely. It may lead to misunderstanding of one's motives, to a not-understanding, and so to non-appreciation, and to all that goes with that. But obedience, simple, full, glad, is the great law of life. Service counts only as it grows out of obedience.

Jesus obeyed fully, perfectly, musically. It was the joy of His heart and life to obey His Father. The commonplaceness of Nazareth mattered not if only the Father's voice said " in whom I am well pleased." The sharpness of the Wilderness conflict, the daily duelling with Jerusalem leaders, the agony of Gethsemane, the awful experience of Calvary, were gladly accepted and even rejoiced in, for they came in the path of obedience to the Father's will.

His obedience was intelligent and full. And the keenness of that remarkable intellect of His —I am speaking of Him just now as a man, all the strength of His tremendous will, all the love of His great heart, were brought to bear on this—obedience to the Father's will.

That implies several things underlying the obedience. It meant a trained ear; an ear trained by listening, trained by study of the Old Testament Scripture, trained by prayer, yes, trained by obedience; for disobedience, failure to obey, dulls and deafens the ear. It meant

study of the Word of God. So there came to
be the clear understanding of the Father's plan.
It meant a discerning mind, a simple, sane sense.
Don't forget the perfect humanness of our divine Lord. He learned His Father's will as we
may learn it—by studying the Word. He was
wondrously familiar with the old Hebrew rolls.
He was saturated, not simply with their teaching, but with their very language. Indeed He
talked in the words of the Bible. It is remarkable how far His talks can be reproduced out
of the Old Testament. He knew it by heart.

Yet remember that knowledge came to Him
in the same way as to any man—namely, by
study, by repeated examination of, and poring
over, and meditation over, and praying over,
the old Hebrew rolls, to which He had access
in Nazareth. That carpenter shop was a study
shop, too. And that obedience meant prayer too.
Through prayer there came the intelligent understanding of the Word of God. Through
prayer there came the grace that enabled Him
to obey.

Obedience never so hard.

And obedience meant a choosing to obey.
There was not simply the general choice to obey.
But as the Father's plan grew in His conscious-
ness bit by bit, He chose to obey at each ad-

vancing step. As He drew on nearer, step by
step, to Gethsemane and Calvary, as there came
in upon Him with terrible realness just what
obedience meant, of pain and shame, He *chose*
to obey. Herein lay the strange power of His
obedience in defeating the evil one; He chose
to obey. His obedience was the result of his
calm repeated choice.

Obedience was the touchstone of all His human career. He lived that humble shut-away
Nazareth life, with its daily round of carpenter
shop, narrow home, intercourse with men who
did not understand Him—He lived so because
so the Father planned. And He obeyed. The
feeding of the hungry five thousand, the raising
of Jairus' daughter, and the raising of Lazarus,
were not greater to Him than the Nazareth
round. All came to Him in the pathway
of obedience. The underlying principle was
obedience.

Yet obedience was never made so hard. The
tempter attended to that. Obedience never
meant so much pain and shame. The tempter
planted that path with thorns, and planted all
the cruelty of a cross directly in its middle. And
obedience was never so joyously given. Jesus
made music by His obedience. Obedience is
the rhythmic melody of a human will keeping
tune with God's. No sweeter music is ever
made.

Obedience took Jesus up the hill of the Cross.
It drew from Him the life-blood that washed out
the blot made by sin on the righteousness of
God, and that redeemed us forever from its
curse. He obeyed though His heart broke in
doing it; and so He has broken our hearts with
His unmatched love. Obedience! Obedience!!
This was the one gripping purpose of His life.
In this he ran exactly counter to the evil one
whose dominant trait is his disobedience. In
his obedience Jesus foiled and defeated the
enemy at every turn till the climax of Calvary
was reached.

Fearlessness.

Now out of these very traits of our Lord's
character grew another trait which was of immense power in the victory over the evil one.
I mean the trait of fearlessness. Jesus was utterly fearless.

Fear is bred of sin. It is as common as sin.
Its influence upon our lives is immense, clear
beyond all our conception. It cripples our
bodies, dulls our minds, stupefies our power of
action, and is a continual drag upon our lives.
If we could be wholly free of any and every
sense of fear we would have new bodies, new
minds, new spirits, new faith, new courage, and
new power. The chains of this slavery wrought
by sin are never out of sight, nor out of earshot.

In being wholly free from sin our Lord was wholly free from all sense of fear. This very fearlessness made Satan fear Him. It lead him boldly on where he felt he should go, utterly regardless of circumstances and of consequences. Once the way of obedience, and of service in obedience, was clear to Him, He went straight ahead regardless of difficulties. This greatly intensified His victory over the evil one. It aided greatly in the crippling of the evil one's attacks upon Him.

The tempter plays upon our sense of fear to an extent that is nothing short of startling. The fear of being in personal want is to-day holding back millions of gold, that, if loosened out as God planned, would utterly change the condition of the whole heathen world, and actually move forward the date upon the calendar when our Lord will return to set up Kingdom conditions over all the earth. It is quite probable that nine-tenths of all our action is controlled by this wrong, slavish, sin-bred sense of fear.

In His utter absence of all sense of fear, and with the simple, unquestioning faith in His Father that would go with that, our Lord was defeating the tempter, and treading down smooth the path of victory for our feet.

Aggressiveness of Love.

The fifth trait also grew up out of the first three. Our Lord was aggressive. He pushed steadily, aggressively on in the way marked out for Him. Fear is cowardly. Faith is aggressive; it finds the right path and then its onward steady moving can't be stopped. Purity is aggressive. The unselfish passion for God has a strange power of aggressiveness. Love is aggressive. Goodness is aggressive. Fearlessness is always on the move forward when the need calls.

Jesus' aggressiveness was tremendous. His mere presence here showed His aggressiveness. Here, where sin reigned, and death and misery and suffering through sin, here He came. Down into the very thick of Satan's sphere of action He deliberately came with His sweet purity and obedience. Into the midst of demon-possessed and diseased men, into the midst of prejudice and superstition and cruelty that sin has bred, He quietly came, and by His very presence attacked all of this work of Satan's hands.

Every added hour of that life of purity was a hard aggressive attack upon the evil one. Every beating of His great heart in compassionate love for the multitude scattered like torn sheep, made aggressive inroad on the tempter's domain. We think that sin is aggressive, and it is. But it can't compare with the steady aggressive energy of goodness and love. The tempter seems to be all aggressiveness, of a very tenacious, persistent sort, especially if you are trying to get away from him. But our Lord Jesus was aggressive in a way that made a new record.

Now dig down under those five words—sinlessness, unselfishness, obedience, fearlessness, and aggressiveness—and you will quickly find the consonants and vowels that spell the one word—love. God is love. Jesus revealed His deity in the love which He lived. Only the word takes on a new meaning, or rather reveals its own true meaning, as He lived it. Love is pure. Love is utter unselfishness. Love is obedient— " he that hath my commandments and keepeth them, he it is that loveth me." [1] Love is fearless—" perfect love casteth out fear." [2] Love is aggressive—" the love of Christ " [3] is an irresistible, constraining force driving us ever onward to meet the needs of men.

It was love as incarnated in Jesus that defeated the prince of hate. This is the secret of victory, love, as its meaning is revealed by Jesus. In all of this our Lord defeated the enemy. He was cutting the ground out from under the enemy's feet. Such a life completely neutralized the tempter. In what He was, and

[1] John xiv. 21.   [2] 1 John iv. 18.   [3] 2 Cor. v. 14.

in what He did, our Lord defeated the evil one at every turn, and left him no possible chance of recovery.

Calvary was the climax. The death was the climax of the life. It gathered up into itself all the meaning of the life. It was the crowning act of the defeat administered to the traitor prince, and of the victory won on our behalf. There the sinless one was made sin for us. In that He forever defeated the prince of sin, and settled His claim upon us. The Cross was the greatest act of unselfishness ever done. And in that fact lies the defeat of the selfish one. The obedience of our Lord's life reached its highest and finest point when He poured out His life-blood with such shame and pain. " He was obedient unto death, yea, the death of the cross." [1]   In that obedience, carried to the farthest possible point against the extreme of difficulties, He defeated the disobedient prince. And he fearlessly and aggressively pushed His victorious way through until the great work of our redemption was completely finished. This is the secret of our Lord's sweeping victory over the tempter.

[1] Philippians ii. 8.

FOR THE OVERCOMERS

A Call out of the Glory.

Our Master has spoken once since He left that group of men, with up-turned faces, on Olivet's top. Out from the glory, His voice comes to us clearly in John's Revelation. That little closing book of the Bible begins with the Master's seven-fold message to His Church.[1] Each part of that message begins with a description of Himself; then He speaks clearly and plainly of what the Church looks like to His searching eye; and then each ends with the ringing cry, " to him that overcometh."

Down from the glory comes this earnest pleading call to us to take up the fight which He began, and to carry it to a finish in the power of His victory. That seven-times repeated " to —him—that—overcometh " tells that the conflict is still on, that each man must settle it for himself, that each of us must overcome or be overcome, and that we may overcome if we will, but it will only be through fighting, and real fighting too.

Our Lord got the victory; He got it only

[1] Revelation ii., iii.

through fighting for it. He means that each of us shall get the victory also. We can get it if we will. We get it through His victory. We stand no chance at all save as we go in the power of what He has done. But even so we get it only through our own fighting for it. We must fight if we would win. There is no other way.

We must fight in the strength of His victory. And each of us must fight as really as though the conflict had not already been decided by Him. Only as we fight can we know victory. If we don't overcome, we shall be overcome. If we don't actively push the fighting, we shall be pushed over into defeat.

Our Lord plans that we shall follow in the victory He has won. Each of us is to be an overcomer. In the upper room that Resurrection evening He said, " As the Father hath sent me, even so send I you." [1] We are to be as He—the same life to live, the same earth to live on, the same earnest service to do, the same enemy to fight, and by His grace the same victory to achieve. We are to be the same sort of man as He, one of whom Satan is afraid, whom he can neither touch nor resist.

[1] John xx. 21.

" Follow Me."

The practical question is, How can you and
I be that sort of a man? Well, the Master has
shown us the secret of victory. We are to be
as He. Let us look at the road He has beaten
down for our feet. You will remember that
there are five finger-posts marking the road.

First of all there must be no sin in us if we
are to be overcomers. Sin is Satan's footing.
He works through the sin in us. There must
be no sin. " But," you say, " that rules us out
at once, for we have all sinned." The answer
to that is very simple—our sin must be put over
upon our Lord Jesus. There was no sin *in*
Him; but there was sin *on* Him—ours. There
is sin both in us and on us. But it can all be
put upon our sin-bearer. We meet this first
condition by trusting the Lord Jesus as Saviour.
There is no sweeter verse in Holy Writ than
this of John's, " the blood of Jesus Christ continually cleanseth from all sin." [1] There is never
a moment when we do not need to trust that
precious bloodshedding of His on account of
our sins.

Out of the midst of that great conflict between the heavenly host under Michael, and the
forces of evil under Satan, with the great victory for Michael that settled it, there comes this

[1] 1 John i. 7.

ringing cry, "they overcame on the ground of the blood of the Lamb."[1]   We can overcome daily by trusting the blood of the Lamb, and only so.   The tempter hates that Name, and that truth, and he flees before it.   When temptation comes to you, claim the power of the blood, and both temptation and tempter will flee.

Then there is a second word to be put in here—It can be true that there is no sin in you as far as the *purpose of your life* is concerned. We can be sinless *in purpose*.   And as we tread that road we shall become more and more free from sin in actual life.   We can choose that sin shall be put out and kept out.   That choice must be daily.   It must control every action of life. It must be as constant as temptation is.

A Narrow Path.

Then there is the second finger-post—there must be no self-seeking in us.   Self-seeking is the Satan-spirit.   Through the self-seeking spirit in us, he gets a free hand to do what he chooses.   And here we are just as helpless in ourselves as on the first item.   Yet there is a way of victory here, too, and not a difficult way for the earnest man.   We can yield the control of our daily life to the Holy Spirit.   The Holy Spirit will burn the old self-spirit out.   The

[1] Revelation xii. 11.

blood of Jesus Christ to wash the sin out, the
fire of the Holy Spirit to burn the self-spirit
out—this is the sure way of victory here;
it is the only way, but it is an unfailing
way.

There needs to be the most rigorous discipline
here. I do not mean in a morbid, extreme way,
but simply a sane, sensible choosing to keep out
of your life whatever comes from this source.
And the quiet daily touch alone with the Master will cultivate your good sense to know what
is to be kept out, or taken in. Whatever of the
old self-spirit is allowed in will make just so
much less the victory of your life.

And the third finger-post is this—simple, full
obedience to the Master's will for you. Obedience is the one pathway of power. We should
serve less and obey more, or rather, we should
do no serving save as it comes in obeying the
Voice. When will the Church learn to put
obedience before service! When it does there
will come new power and new triumphs.

Yet, mark keenly, obedience to be intelligent
and wise means a *clear vision*. Moses, killing
the Egyptian, was zealous, but he hadn't a clear
vision. Paul, persecuting the Christians was full
of zeal, but he hadn't a clear vision? Elijah depressed under the juniper tree, Peter refusing
to eat with the Gentile Christians at Antioch—
these men were earnest, but they lacked the

clear vision.   The secret of victory is this—a
clear vision of God's purposes, and of His plan
for you, and then a faithful steady unflinching
obedience to that vision.   The tempter can do
nothing with or against the man who obeys.
This is a sure road to victory.

Pushing Bravely on.

And the fourth finger-post to the victory-road
is *fearlessness*.   Nothing weakens us like fear.
Nothing weakens the tempter in his assaults
upon us like a quiet, bold, steady fearlessness.
Satan can't operate in an atmosphere of trust;
it chokes him.   God cannot act in an atmosphere
of fear; it hinders Him.   One of the commonest
phrases on the lips of God throughout this Bible
is this, "Fear not."   Like a bit of sweet in-
spiriting music it runs throughout these pages.
And, if He may have His way it will be the
unfailing music of our lives.   "Fear not," is
His continual word to you and me.

No matter how tight the corner, how steep
the road, and how rough, how difficult the circumstance, however fearsome the growling of
the tempter—yet *"fear not."*   Let this be the
continual song of your life.   The tempter can't
stand up before a fearless spirit.   And there
is no need for fear; our Lord is Victor.   He has
all power.   And His power is at our disposal.

There is *always need of prayer, but never cause for fear.*

That Revelation cry of victory has a tremendous second clause to it. "They overcame on the ground of the blood of the Lamb, and because of the word of their testimony." [1] Their voice rang out clear, and boldly fearless. The human was coupled with the divine. The testimony made the overcoming power of the blood effective. Bold, wise fearlessness in life and speech, in action and spirit, undercuts the power of the tempter.

And the fifth finger-post needs sharp emphasis. There must be aggressive warfare against the evil one. I do not mean by "aggressive," making a noise and raising clouds of dust, but the steady on-moving of the sun in its course. I mean the aggressiveness of love, of sunshine, of goodness. There needs to be the fearless standing up against the wiles of the tempter. We should get our fighting clothes on and well-girded too, for sharp decisive action.

There is a good deal of meek submission by Christian people that is both cowardly and sinful. What comes along is yielded to as God's will. Whereas a great deal of what comes along is not His will, but is the result of the planning of the evil one. Aggression means a thinking keenly into God's way of working, a seeing

[1] Revelation xii. 11.

clearly what is His will, and what is opposed to His will, and then a vigorous resisting in the Victor's Name of anything not God's will.

We should be ambitious to be able to repeat dear old Paul's words at the end of his strenuous life, " I have fought the good fight." [1] There's great need of more fighters, wise, steady, sane, hard fighters against the evil one, in Jesus' great Name.

> " Ne'er think the victory won
> Nor lay thine armour down;
> Thine arduous task will not be done
> Till thou obtain the crown."

That victorious cry of Michael's host has still another clause, " They overcame him on the ground of the blood of the Lamb, and because of the word of their testimony, *and* they loved not their life even unto death." There was the aggressiveness of sacrifice. There is nothing so aggressive in the fight against the evil one as the sacrificial spirit of love, that counts not its own life a thing to be prized in order that victory may come.

Overcoming Armour.

Paul gives a fine picture of the overcoming man. It is in the last chapter of the Ephesian

[1] 2 Timothy iv. 7.

Epistle.[1] He describes first the foe against
which we are to fight. Then follows the description of God's fighting man. The overcomer
must be a fighter. The victory comes only
through conflict. Notice God's fighting man—
"having girded your loins with truth." That
is, a clear, simple grasp of God's truth as revealed in His Word. It means such a grasp of
it as grips the life, girds the loins, and puts you
into fit shape for vigorous action.

Then follows this: "Having put on the breast-
plate of righteousness." There must be a clean
pure life. The truth has girded so tightly that
the advance of sin has been fought off. "And
having shod your feet with the preparation of
the gospel of peace," or having the gospel as a
sure footing in your fighting. That is, a clear
grasp of the essence of the Gospel, namely, that
salvation is through the blood of the Lamb, and
only so—this is the only sure footing for this
fight. Any other will fail you in the thick smoke
and din of the battle.

"Withal taking up the shield of faith." A
strongly simple, childlike faith in God is the sure
defence against the attacks of the enemy. "The
helmet of salvation" is a clear unshakeable as-
surance of one's own personal salvation. There
can be no effective fighting while any doubt of
this lingers. "The sword of the Spirit" is the

[1] Ephesians vi. 10-19.

good strong grasp of the truth, for the enemy, when he tries the Wilderness tactics on you, as well as for your service among men. And the description closes with the chief emphasis on prayer.

Leaving Paul's armour figure aside, those seven things might be put into this simple shape. First, dependence upon the blood of Jesus Christ, which is the whole of the gospel of peace. A continual claiming of the power of His death and resurrection. Second, a pure, holy life. Third, obedience based upon an intelligent grasp of the Word. Fourth, fearless aggressiveness both in attack and defence. And then underlying and overlapping, and breathing through all the rest, a spirit of quiet confident praying. This sort of a man will be an overcomer. There will be sure victory for him at every onward step of the way. He will fight and he will win.

And mark you keenly, all of this is entirely practicable and possible through grace. The Holy Spirit is living in you and me, wherever the door has swung for Him. He has come in, partly, to make us good fighters and overcomers. He can be depended upon to do it, too. Our part is to yield intelligently and actively to His generalship.

There is great need for more overcomers, and our Lord earnestly calls from the glory for men to follow in His steps and His strength. He won the decisive victory over our enemy. But every man must make that victory his own on the battlefield of his own life. And in Jesus' great Name we can, and, please God, by His great sweet grace we will.

FIGHTING TACTICS: THE TEMPTER'S AND OURS

Recognition half the Fight.

An attacking enemy unrecognized has his battle half won. Recognition is a long step toward His defeat. If we know something of the tempter's way of fighting it will be an immense help in recognizing and resisting and defeating him. Our Lord Jesus was victorious in the Wilderness, partly, because He was keen in recognizing the tactics used against Himself. His keenness in recognizing made him quicker in resisting.

The tempter has one of two aims in coming to us. First and most of all, he wants to get us away, and keep us away from God. That is his first aim, of course. But there is a second aim, which has not been recognized so quickly or so much. It is against those of us who are Christians. No small part of his effort is directed against those of us who want to be true. And the thing he is driving at there is to steal away our peace and our power.

There are many who would not do anything they know to be displeasing to the Master. They conscientiously guard that side of their lives. The tempter's favourite mode of approach with such is to steal away their sweet peace of mind and heart. For in stealing away peace, he is also stealing much of their power. There can be fulness of power going out, only as there is fulness of peace within.

And he is also constantly trying to take away our power directly, or to make it less so far as possible. By sin, by selfishness in some subtle shape, by attacks upon bodily conditions, by making us tired, or depressed, or discouraged, or switching us on to some side track, he can do much to switch us off from the full touch with God, through which only can come fulness of power in life and service. If we are to enjoy full peace of heart, and a steady even poised course of action full of God's power, we must know something of the tempter's fighting tactics, and be prepared to meet and match him constantly.

Let me begin with just a word about his tactics against us corporately. He is a keen fighter against the Church as a whole. The main thing he is driving at here is to divide the Church. He is an adept at divisive tactics. Under one cover or another he aims to separate one body of believers from the others. He knows the tremendous power there is in unity. He knows so well the resistless power against himself of united prayer, of united action, of a united spirit controlling, that he has done his utmost to kill that spirit of unity.

I do not mean to speak disparagingly of the term, when I say that Satan is a keen theologian. Anything of any sort that divides the Church, or splits up any group of Christ's followers, suits his purposes. And in saying that I am not now pleading for a universal unity of churches, for unity sometimes means dishonour: Loyalty to the essential Gospel of our Lord, and to His person, will prevent the union that is sometimes thought of.

Two Lines of Approach.

But the chief thing we are to talk together about now is his tactics in dealing with us personally. And here he has two avenues of approach—he tempts, and he attacks. The temptation is an attempt to induce us to do wrong, to lead us, by much or by little, aside from the one right path. The attack is an attempt to injure us regardless of our consent. He tempted Eve in Eden. He attacked Job. He did both with our Lord. Every weapon at command was used against Him. Jesus met every sort of temptation and attack on our behalf. He was tempted in the Wilderness, and when the Greeks came. He was attacked by that unusually violent Galilean storm; and in Gethsemane, and on Calvary.

The temptation is for all, the attack is for those resisting the temptation. When he fails in tempting, he tries attacking. Of course it is true that the attack itself may become, and often does become, simply a subtler form of temptation. It throws a flood of light upon the character of Job that he was attacked by Satan. Those attacks told this story, that Job had been tempted and had resisted. He had become skilled in recognizing and fighting the tempter's temptations. Then the tempter, having failed so largely there, cunningly changes his line of approach.

In temptation he seeks our consent to his proposals. In his attacks he does what he is allowed to, acting within the limitations set by God, to injure without seeking our consent. So the attack itself becomes a temptation, usually a temptation to doubt God, or to depart from the path of obedience in seeking our own comfort or ease or protection. The attack is really the second hard drive when temptation fails.

In these temptations and attacks, he is sometimes subtle, like a snake crawling along in the tall grass to strike its fangs in when you least think it is there. Sometimes he comes with the rush of a sudden wild storm down the valley, in an attempt to sweep you off your feet.

The Outworks.

Now notice, please, the rule he follows in these temptations and attacks. He always aims at the weakest point; that is by weakest I mean the point where he is most likely to succeed. If successful there, of course, his point is achieved. If defeated at that point of approach he proceeds to the next likeliest, and so on. In Eden his first approach was successful. It is rather humiliating that our oldest kinsman yielded at the first point of approach. In the Wilderness he went from one point to another, until having failed in each he was obliged to leave. But note, too, that though he may fail at some one point of approach, he is sure to come back to that same point in some changed guise.

It is always good tactics for us to guard our weak points, or our likeliest points of approach. And as a man's strong point is quite likely to become his weak point through over-confidence, therefore guard all points, but especially the weak, the likeliest points of approach.

Then mark that it is a favourite method with the tempter to come through our bodies. He tempts through the natural appetites and desires. He attacks through weakness or sickness or disease. Eve was tempted first by the appeal to a perfectly proper bodily desire. When that temptation was yielded to, the next came likewise in the realm of the body, to use a proper function for a purpose not intended.

Our Lord was tempted first in the appeal to His sense of hunger. It was a bodily temptation. It is striking that the tempter made no headway with Job until he attacked his body. Job remained true through the disasters that came by war, and storm, by loss of children and property, but when his body was touched his strength of resistance began to weaken.

Many a man who would scorn to yield to what he recognizes as a sin in the bodily realm will over-use his bodily strength in doing God's service, or will eat imprudently, or eat such things as are not wholesome, not thinking of these as temptations. But the result is that he is either weakened in his work, or set aside from doing it. And that is, at least, a partial victory for the tempter. When we come to realize that whatever weakens our bodies is a temptation to be resisted, we shall have gone far in defeating the evil one, at one of his subtlest points of approach.

Attacking the Citadel.

Another common mode of approach is *through the mind.* First, there is the indirect approach to the mind. Whatever weakens the body, by so much robs us likewise of mental strength. I

know that it has been commonly said that some
of the most saintly men have had weak bodies.
But I am quite clear that their saintliness was not
due to their weak bodies, but in spite of them. If
God may have His way, we will have strong
bodies as well as saintly lives. There is no
temptation or attack harder to resist than that
which comes through or to the body.

Then there is the direct approach to the mind.
The commonest form here is to make us over-
pleased with ourselves and with what we have
done. Egotism is one of the commonest of all
vices. The undue sense of our own importance
or ability can get in through a very thin crevice,
and does. Yet this is a bit of the very core
of the Satan-spirit. The line between a proper
self-esteem, and an improper thinking more
highly of ourselves than we ought to think, is
a very thin line, very easily crossed, indeed very
hard not to cross.

Only an eye fixed steadily upon Him, who
gave us all we have, and to whom we are in
debt to do the very best we can with our abili-
ties—only that steady watching of His face will
keep our feet steady too, and keep our heads
from getting dizzy, when the path leads up some
unusual height, with a crowd watching.

But there are other modes of attack upon us
through our minds. And I want to speak more
fully of these both because they are so very

common, and because they are not recognized as coming from the tempter. Mental depression is a favourite mode of attacking Christians, especially those who earnestly desire to ring true. There is a good bit of mental depression without doubt due directly to bodily conditions. But there is also a great deal that comes directly from the evil one or from some of his numerous messenger spirits.

This depression may be found in all degrees of intensity, from the slightest which yields to help, on to the degree of severe melancholy that leads to insanity, and the taking of one's life. It may begin with a sense of loss of peace, a sense of God's presence being withdrawn, as though He were displeased and had left us. The quiet hour of prayer seems mechanical; the heart seems cold, and these very feelings deepen and intensify the sense of depression. While much of this may be traced to bodily conditions, without doubt much of it is a direct attack by an unrecognized evil spirit who is seeking to rob us of peace and power.

Here recognition is half of the remedy, and if it lead to quick resistance in Jesus' Name, the relief will be complete. I recall talking with a Christian lady from Europe, a highly cultured lady of noble birth, whose service has been greatly blest of God to large numbers, but who was suffering from mental depression to a de-

gree that was painful.   Recognition of the evil
spirit at work, and resistance in the Victor's
Name, quickly cleared the sky for the bright
shining of the sun again.

Obsession.

Sometimes the attack takes the form of mental stupidity or the sense of extreme tiredness
when reading the Bible, or praying, or attempt-
ing some bit of Christian service.   I recall an
earnest Christian woman of much more than
usual mental keenness, who for a long time was
troubled in this way.   Her mind was clear
enough with other matters or books, but when
she turned for her Bible reading, she grew mentally stupid, and seemed unable to get anything.
She would kneel to pray at night and intense
sleepiness would come over her, yet when she
would rise from her knees, and retire for the
night, sleep would leave her eyes.   And this continued long until a bit of light broke.   She recognized that the evil one, or an evil spirit, was
attacking her.   And steady resistance in Jesus'
Name brought relief which has continued without break.   And this is only one instance of
many of the same sort that I have known of
personally.

I know an earnest Christian whose service
has been much used and blest, who was beset

with an abnormal sense of tiredness, which held
him back from service, and affected what service
he did.   No extra sleeping nor resting brought
relief, but as quickly as he was led to see that
he was being attacked by evil forces, he resisted
earnestly and aggressively in the great Name,
and he quickly entered into a new life of peace
of heart, and of renewed vigorous mental
activity.

I want to say a word here about what is
called obsession. We are more familiar with
the term demon-possession than with the companion term demon-obsession. Demon-possession means that a demon or evil spirit has been
allowed to come in and take possession of one's
personality. That was extremely common in the
Gospel days, and is still very common in non-
Christian lands, and much more common in
Christian lands than is commonly supposed.

This other thing of demon-obsession is extremely common too, though not much recognized. It simply means that evil spirits are
attacking and disturbing and annoying us.
Demon-possession is impossible without the consent of the man whose personality is taken possession of. But obsession is possible without
such consent, because it is an *outer* attack. And
the remarkable thing is that obsession by demons
is quite a common experience by the saintliest
people, though so rarely recognized. Indeed it

seems to be true that it is the earnest, conse-
crated, saintly ones who are singled out for this
form of attack.   Whatever disturbance or an-
noyance an evil spirit may cause in this way,
comes under this general head of obsession.   The
mental depression, the melancholia, and mental
stupidity, and tiredness, of which I have spoken,
really belong under this head of obsession.   But
it also takes more vigorous forms than these.

Some Actual Experiences.

I recall the experience of a man of matured
years and well-seasoned judgment.   He had
been led to take an advance step in his Christian
life which meant much of sacrifice.   He has
since then been used in his Christian service in
a marked way, and to an unusual degree.   This
experience came just after the step referred to
had been taken.   He was awakened in the night
by the sense of an unwholesome presence in the
room, or rather the feeling that the room was
full of evil beings.   A peculiar feeling of horror
came over him, with strange bodily sensations.
The air of the room seemed stifling.   He quickly
recognized that he was being attacked, rose from
bed, and attempted to sing a verse of a hymn
with Jesus' Name in.   It seemed impossible at
first to get his lips open, or any sound out.   But
he persisted and soon the soft singing was clear

and full, and the spirit atmosphere of the room
cleared at once. And with grateful heart he lay
down again, and slept sweetly until the morning. Yet he is a man of unusual caution, with
a critical matter-of-fact spirit of investigation.

A friend was telling recently of a somewhat
similar experience. He is an earnest godly man,
of mature experience, and more than the aver-
age sanity of judgment. It was shortly after
retiring for the night, and before sleep had come,
that a peculiar sense of awful blackness came
over him. With the strange sense of mental
keenness that marks such experiences he seemed
to know that his mind was slipping away from
his control. He could not recall who he was,
and realized that he could not. He could not
even remember his name. There was an overwhelming sense of blackness, as though his mind
were saturated with a blackness that was pressing in upon him. And he said he was conscious
of being conscious of only one thnig—the Name
of Jesus. He clung to that, saying the Name
"Jesus" over and again. It was as though
every power of thought and speech was gone
save that of uttering that Name. Relief came,
and with a sense of gratitude that could never
be told, he said, he prayed and went to sleep.

I could repeat many such experiences that
have come to my knowledge. These will be
sufficient to make clear my meaning in talking

of obsession. Evil spirits attack the saintliest
men and women, in these and similar ways.
Failure to recognize the nature and source of
the attack has sometimes led to serious results.

I recall one of the most brilliant, brainy men
that ever preached the Gospel, a man of unusual
charm of personality and earnest devotion, whose
life went abruptly out under the touch of his
own hand. The physician used the phrase "intense melancholia." But careful study into the
case revealed the fact that without question the
fuller explanation can be found here in demon-
obsession, unrecognized.

These are some of the tempter's fighting tactics. They are given here that we may be
quicker and keener to recognize him and his,
and so to resist more quickly and successfully
in the Name of his Victor, which he so fears.

"On the Ground of the Blood."

And now we want to talk a bit on the other
side—our fighting tactics. What are the true
tactics which this enemy of ours fears and cannot resist. There will be a little repetition here
of what has been said before. But repetition
is the law of deep and lasting impression.

First of all must come that great statement
made of Michael's fight and victory in John's
Revelation. "They overcame him on the ground

of the blood of the Lamb." [1] We cannot get
beyond that. The enemy is the same, the fight
the same, and the means of victory the same too.
It was by the shedding of His own blood that
our Lord Jesus Himself defeated the enemy.
It is only by that same precious blood that we
can get victory too.

This seems like strange fighting, not spear
and sword, not gun-cotton and powder but—a
Name, the Name of Jesus; a fact, the fact that
He gave His blood for us. They overcame on
the ground of the blood of the Lamb; so may
we. And only so, can we. There must be the
daily pleading of the power of the blood, the
claiming of its redeeming power from all the
power of the enemy. In the thick of the hardest fighting that blood-red banner persistently
flung out will rout this foe. We never get beyond the need of claiming the power of that
blood.

Then the second chapter in our book of tactics must be this; habitual surrender to the mastery of our Lord Jesus. Only so can there be
the fighting that wins. Anything else is letting
the enemy within the lines. That surrender
must be full and sane and sensible; it must be
rhythmic with the glad music of our hearts.
It must be habitual, as habitual as breathing.

It must cover the bodily habits, the mental

[1] Revelation xii. 11.

life, the social contacts, the friendships, the business relations and methods, and even that strangely clinging, subtle stuff called money. A glad cheery yielding of the whole life to the mastery of the Lord Jesus, this is splendid fighting tactics, and irresistible. But anything less means loss of power for us, and gain of power by our foe.

Then there is a daily prayer that our Victor has given us to use—" deliver us from the evil one." It is striking that that is one of the few petitions in the Lord's prayer. It is to be repeated daily, as the language of the prayer makes clear. The old reading is, " deliver us from evil," but it seems clearly to be the fuller meaning of the Master's language to make it personal—" *the* evil *one*." And the word " deliver " has all the force of the word " rescue." Our Master teaches us daily to bow and pray, " rescue me from the evil one." It is most significant.

I know a thoughtful man who begins the day by quietly slipping his hands over his body from head down, slowly repeating this prayer, " deliver me from the evil one, and breathe in afresh Thy own life, in Jesus' great Name." That is good fighting tactics. It is insisting on all the powers of our Victor's victory, in the stress and thick of life's need.

"*The Sword of the Spirit.*"

There is a fourth bit in our fighting tactics that needs much emphasis, namely, saturate your mind with the Word of God. Let there be a quiet time daily alone with the Book, until you get full of it, and then fuller. Let the Book itself have first place in that quiet time. No book, however good, and no collection of verses, however choice, should be allowed to take this first place. Let the reading be wide, by the page; let it be daily, through the year, with sometimes a bit extra, but never a bit less; let it be prayerful with the heart held open to God's own touch. So will come the familiarity and clear vision so essential. This was our Lord's method in meeting the tempter in the Wilderness.

And this leads directly to the fifth thing I want to emphasize strongly. It is this, cultivate a sane judgment, and a quiet mind. One should pray daily for the blessing of a sound mind, one that does not go to extremes. Nothing cultivates the judgment like this Word of God, interpreted to us by the Holy Spirit. Avoid extremes, both the extreme of over-cautiousness, and the extreme of radicalism.

Faith Street is on a hill. It lies very close to two other streets, one at each end leading downward. The one is Queer Street; the other is Doubt Street. You want to avoid each extreme.

Live on the top of the hill with clearness of vision, sanity of judgment, and quietness of mind. This will help greatly in actively fighting the enemy. Satan does not like poise, he prefers the pendulum swing.

A sixth point has been referred to repeatedly, but must be given the emphasis of a place in this grouping. I mean this, learn to recognize the enemy's approach, whether he comes himself or through one of his numerous messenger-spirits. Cultivate a keen ear for his voice and step, a quick eye for his hand, however gloved, and a sensitive spirit for his touch and presence. We are to take time a little later to talk together about the tempter's disguises, and how to detect them. That, I hope, will help us in this work of quick and sure recognition. Without doubt our Lord's keenness and quickness in recognizing both tempter and temptation in the Wilderness was an immense help in the victory won there. Yet that recognition came to him in the same way as it may come to us.

The Wondrous Name.

And then a last word must be put in for the hour of stress. When the temptation comes so subtly, and crowds so hard, remember this word—claim Christ's victory. Remember that the victory *has been* won. Claim that victory as your own. Go in the strength of what Some-body else has done. The victory you are need-ing just now, when the temptation comes with a wild rush, and nearly sweeps you off your feet at once, remember that victory has been won. It is an accomplished fact. Claim it as your own, and it will be your own in fact. There is far more victory just within grasp than you have realized. Reach out your hand and take as your very own what has been done for you.

That victory has been enshrined in a Name. All the power of the Nazareth victory, and of the Wilderness victory, all the power of the great climax victory of Calvary, and of the Resurrection morning—all is packed into one word, a Name, the Name of Jesus. There is far more, infinitely more practical help and power in that Name than we have dreamed of; certainly far more than we have ever used. The Name of Jesus is the most valuable asset of the Christian life.

I remember a young man coming up to me at the close of a service in London. He told me of how sorely he had been tempted, how he seemed to make no headway against the strug-gle in his Christian life, until the suggestion came to him of the practical value of that Name above every name. Instantly he began using it, reverently, prayerfully, eagerly, and relief and victory came. And the look of eye and face

revealed how real was the victory and peace that
had come to him.

A missionary in South Africa has told a story
of her experience in the use of that great Name.
The story has a simplicity and a power, that
makes one feel all afresh that we have not used
that great Name as we may and should.   She
was travelling in Bechuanaland, camping by the
banks of a badly swollen river.   The discom-
forts of heavy rains, bad roads, poor food, and
stinging insects were very great.   But sorer far
was the moral havoc being wrought within sight,
by the wayside canteen where liquors were sold
to the hundreds of poor dark-skinned natives.
The distress of the situation seemed unbearable.
In her almost despair of soul she was drawn
away to pray, then in calmer mood was led to
go over toward the canteen.

Her thought was directed to one man, very
old, very poor, clad in a few filthy rags, with a
bloated face, bleared eyes, and loathsome sores,
all the result of his drinking the cheap adul-
terated liquor kept in the canteen.   He was just
staggering towards the canteen when she called
him.   And as he stopped to speak with her, she
asked him why he drank when it was ruining
him.

With a wild laugh he said, " Why? I can't
help it.   I am enslaved by this vile white man's
drink.   I would gladly quit, but I can't."   And

she told him there was a way out into freedom from his slavery. It was in a name. "A name," he said with a touch of awe coming over him. "Yes, a name," she said. And would she tell him that name. Praying for guidance, she told him as simply as she could the story of the Gospel, and of the power in the Name of Jesus. And the old black wreck repeated the Name, *Jesus,* which was but a new sound to him. And they knelt in prayer among the trees and parted.

Her journey took her away, but weeks after, on returning, she met the old black man's wife, and from her gleaned the fascinating sequel to the story. The poor old enslaved heathen man had gone away, and when the fever for drink came upon him, he had with great earnestness repeated the Name of Jesus over and over. And in his simple speech, the fever left him, the craving for the drink went away, and he felt as if he had never tasted the stuff. He said his mouth felt clean as a little child's, and his body had become strong and well.

One day he had allowed an old drinking companion to persuade him to go with him. As they started toward the canteen, the old fever for drink came upon him. He could feel it burning within his body. He tried to break away from his companion, but the old slavery gripped him anew and held him fast. Then he remembered, and with all the earnestness of his soul he repeated the Name over, " Jesus, *Jesus,* JESUS." And he said, " A coolness came over my brain, and my body, and I was free again, and turned quickly away."

The meagreness of the man's knowledge of the Gospel makes the story seem almost startling. But the earnestness of his purpose, and the simplicity of his faith, fully made up for lack of knowledge, and supplied the sure link with the Lord Jesus, and through that link the power came in the hour of his sore distress.

I have no doubt that if spirit-beings were visible, any one standing by watching the old black man, would have seen evil spirits hanging about and haunting him, and driving him on in his mad thirst for the drink; and then fleeing, frightened and terrified, before the Name of their Victor, as the old man repeated it, over and again so earnestly.

Fearless Cheer.

The Name that brought the old heathen quick relief from bodily appetite is available for every sort of need, and in every sort of emergency. It is our strong tower into which we can run and be safe. Satan hates that Name. He fears it. All the victory of Nazareth, and the Wilderness, of Calvary, and the Resurrection, is bound up in that Name. And now it is ours

to use. The Master has bequeathed to us the
right to use that Name, and as we do there is
as much and as sure victory for us as there was
gotten by Him.

There is a last word that ought to be put in.
It should be used as a sort of bright underscoring to all that has been said, and to all that will
be said. It will affect the spirit of all our life,
and of all our fighting. It is a word from our
Master's own lips. It comes to us out of the
darkness of the darkest night He knew. In that
exquisitely quiet voice of His he said, " Be of
good cheer; I have overcome." [1] Out of the
gloom of that betrayal night it shines as a bright
gleam of light. It stands out against the back-
ground of the betrayal of a sacred friendship
trust, as a beam of God's own sunshine out
of black storm clouds.

" Be of good cheer "—the uplift of its music
is immense. Let the joyous music of His victory ring its melody in your soul, and then let
the gladness of it out in all your life. Be cheery!
Sing as you fight. Be joyous as you push on.
There is an enemy; yes, but he is defeated. He
is still free to fight; yes, but every fight is meant
to mean a fresh defeat for him. We are living
on the battlefield; yes, but it is to be a victory-
field for us, because of our Leader. The tempter
is cunning and persistent; yes, but he is a

[1] John xvi. 33.

whipped foe. The enemy is more than a match for us; yes, but he has been fairly outmatched by our Lord Jesus. Cheer up! Fasten the flag at the top of the mast, and nail it there, and clinch the nails, cut away the ropes; the flag, the Victor's flag, is there to stay.

"Be of good cheer; *I*." With that glad ringing cry of cheer, couple the personality of Him who gives it to us—"Be of good cheer; *I*." It is because of Him that we can be of good cheer. He is the basis of the cheer. Let this be our constant fighting cry, "Be of good cheer; *I*—"

THE TEMPTER'S DISGUISES AND HOW TO DETECT THEM

Working under Cover.

A disguise is a lie. Its purpose is to deceive. It is something bad hiding its face behind something good. The bad of itself would not have any chance if it came barefaced. It would be refused admittance at once. And if it insisted on getting in would be booted out vigorously. So it steals some good to hide behind. It pretends to be as good as the good. The door is opened for the good, and the bad sneaks stealthily in to carry out its plans.

A disguise is a counterfeit. It aims to make things look different from what they are, and to look better. There are, of course, make-believe disguises used in play in carrying out a part; but these only make it more emphatic that the purpose of a disguise is to deceive.

Now it is a marked charactertistic of the tempter that he uses disguises. It is a most significant characteristic. It puts him at once in sharp contrast with God. God is always in the open. At times He conceals His glory. But that is not that He may hold back something

from us, but that we may the better take in
what is revealed of Himself.   Too much light
blinds, and the blinded eyes get nothing.   A
carefully shaded light, restraining the excessive
brightness, enables us to see more, and to know
what we can't see by what we do see.   God is always in the open.   Our Lord Jesus said to His
accusers, " I have spoken openly."   He was contrasting His openness with the secrecy with
which they stole upon Him under cover of
night to arrest Him, and which also marked His
trial.

Satan works under cover.   It is immensely
suggestive of his character and purposes.   In
Eden he came behind the covering of the most
intelligent and beautiful of all the lower animal
creation.   He is seldom mentioned by name in
the Old Testament.   That is a bit of the faithfulness of its description of things as they actually are.   He carefully conceals his personality, but his disguises can be found all through
the Book, and all through the book of life.   His
footprints are easily found in every roadway of
life.

In the story of Job, it is noteworthy that Job
supposed that all the suffering that came had
been sent directly by God.   It is true that it
had been allowed by God, for a purpose, but it
had not been sent by Him.   But so skilfully had
the actual instigator of Job's troubles worked,

that the suffering man actually mistook him for God.

The tempter is bad; he is only bad; he is bad clear through; he has no spots of good, nor any spurts of good. He is bold as well as bad. He is as bold as He is bad. He hides behind God. The worst hides behind the best. Satan uses God's roads. He never makes roads. His boldness is startling in its daring. He is as blasphemous in his unblushing boldness as in his unmixed badness.

We want to talk in a very simple way about some of the disguises which the tempter uses. We need keener eyes to pierce through the disguise to the real thing underneath. Satan is a rare expert in make-up. He is deceiving even the very elect of God. He has great skill in new disguises when the old ones are found out. It takes keen watching and habitual praying, much study of God's Word, and a God-guided judgment if we are to detect and avoid his disguises, and yet be controlled by a sane, poised common sense in all our daily relations and contracts.

Hiding Behind Natural Desires.

Mark first of all this: *the tempter hides behind natural appetites and desires.* There are certain bodily, and mental, and social, functions

and appetites and desires with which we have
been endowed. The appetite for food and drink;
the sense of taste that appreciates fine flavours;
the longing for and delight in personal companionship; the desire to fit into the scheme of
life and play one's full part in it; the sense of
beauty that can appreciate and enjoy and be
uplifted by the beautiful in landscape and in
artistic handiwork—these are perfectly natural
tastes and desires.

The tempter comes along these natural path-
ways of our being. He prefers such roads.
They make easier travel for him. He seeks
to push us to an extreme, this way or that, in
satisfying these natural desires. He appealed
to Eve's sense of beauty, her sense of taste,
and her desire for knowledge. Had he openly
told her why he had come, and what the result
of her following his suggestion would be, she
would have promptly turned away. But behind
these disguises she was deceived, and so fell into
the tangling snare laid at her feet.

The approach to Job was very cunning. The
aim of the tempter was to make Job doubt God's
love. He came up behind Job's love for his
home, for his children, and for peace and prosperity. This was a perfectly natural love, im-
planted in Job's heart by God. The impression
made upon Job was that God was taking away
his children, breaking up his home, and taking

away his peace and prosperity. The natural
tendency was to have his sense of trust in
God rudely shocked. The approach of the
tempter was behind those natural God-given
desires.

In the Wilderness the first approach of the
tempter was behind a bodily need. The desire
for food was a right thing, of course. The
tempter sought to use a right desire to make our
Lord do that which it would have been wrong
for Him to do, because contrary to His Father's
plan at that time. The second approach was
through something yet higher up. Our Lord
said He would trust the Father to care for His
bodily needs. Through that spirit of trust in
God's loving watch-care the tempter comes up
with his second proposal. Our Lord refused
to go to the extreme of a foolhardy going where
He had not been led.

Again, the third approach was hidden behind
a natural desire. World-wide dominion was a
perfectly natural thing for our Lord Jesus. It
was doubly so. As a man merely He had a
right to such dominion, even such as was given
to Adam, and lost by him. As the new head
of the race all things had been given into His
hands.[1] But he would take possession of his
world-wide dominion in His Father's way, and
time, and only so.[2] The approach was behind

[1] Matthew xi. 27   [2] Ephesians i. 20, 21.

a true natural instinct, the desire for world-wide dominion.

So the tempter is still doing. It is one of his settled ways of coming to us. Along the path of what is right he comes to push us to some extreme, and especially to push us from the narrow path of obedience to the Father's plan, and way, and time. Our safety lies in remembering that every right desire is to be used only for our Father's glory and as He guides.

The natural desire is never to be an end in itself. It is to be used only as a means to a high end. That end is to carry out God's purposes, and reveal the more His glory. The tempter continually tries to sway us over to using these proper natural desires as ends in themselves. The one thing he is driving at is to sway us away from God's plan by little or by much. It is a cunning disguise.

Hiding Behind Men.

Then mark that *the tempter disguises his approach to us behind men*. I do not mean bad men necessarily. I mean that quite unconsciously to themselves he uses good men in ways that will work out his purposes. That word "unconsciously" should be underscored. There

are four illustrations of this sort of thing in the
life of our Lord Jesus.

The first is the coming to Him of His mother
and brethren to seek an interview while He is
in the midst of teaching the multitude.[1]   It
seems to be a strange incident.   It occurs at
the time when the opposition to Him by the
Jerusalem leaders had reached the aggressive
stage.   They were following Him up into Galilee, hounding His steps, and trying by every
sort of means to hinder and, if possible, stop
His work.   Their opposition had reached the
point of danger to Him.   For a second time it
is said that He " withdrew " from the area of
their activity.   That word " withdrew " is a significant one, indicating the seriousness of the
danger threatening Him.   The awful charge of
Satanic collusion had been made against Him.
This setting of the story should be kept in mind.

One day as He is teaching in the midst of a
great crowd an interruption occurs.   Strangely
enough it is a message sent in to Him that His
mother and brethren are on the outskirts of the
crowd and desire an interview.   It is wholly
probable from the records that they had free
access to Him ordinarily, when they were where
He was.   Why this unexpected breaking in while
He is at His work?   It looks very much as
though the leaders had been cunningly working

[1] Matthew xii. 46-50; Mark iii. 31-35; Luke viii. 19-21.

upon her mother heart. They would use her influence to side-track Him. Surely such a fine-grained man as He clearly is will be open to His mother's influences and to her fears and wishes. It was an appeal to a natural love. It touched the tenderest earthly tie our Master had. He revealed a tender solicitude for His mother amid the pain and distress of hanging upon the cross.

It looks very much like an approach by the tempter behind the tender relation existing between Him and His mother. She, of course, would be wholly unconscious that it was so. Only so can His words in reply to the request be fully understood, " Who is my mother? " and so on. He evidently recognized the interruption as something serious. His reply in effect is this: " My mission is not subject to earthly human ties, even though as tender as that of a mother. My relation to my Father is the one controlling purpose and passion of my life." The doing of the Father's will was higher than any human tie or relationship. It is not the first time, nor the last, that the tempter has come behind the sacred, tender tie of kinship.

The second of these is the story of the enthusiastic multitudes over this Man, who could supply bread enough for their hunger.[1] The

[1] John vi. 1-15; with Matthew xiv. 13-22; Mark vi. 30-45.

violent taking off of His Herald, John, led Jesus
to seek a bit of quiet solitude for prayer and
thinking. The end was drawing sharply nearer
in this event. The multitudes invade His pri-
vacy. He patiently teaches, and then feeds the
vast crowd with the few loaves and fishes. The
crowd is completely swept off its feet by His
graciousness and power, and by the sense of
inner physical comfort. Their leaders seem to
have actually conferred with the disciples, and
to have gotten their consent to the proposed
plan of making Jesus King. For the Master
was compelled to " constrain " them to get into
the boat and leave.[1]

They propose a great popular uprising to pro-
claim Jesus King. It may seem to us like an
immature, weak movement. Yet, if such a thing
can be imagined as our Lord taking advantage
of such a thing, it would have undoubtedly become a most formidable movement. At any
rate it was clearly a repetition of the old Wilderness temptation of world-wide dominion
without suffering. Many a Christian leader has
yielded to that sort of a temptation. All unconsciously to themselves, the tempter was coming up behind these multitudes in their pathetic
need, with the old temptation under new guise.

[1] Matthew xiv. 22.

The Subtlest yet.

The third of these is when our Lord first tells the inner circle of the awful experiences ahead to which He would yield.[1] Peter is startled and strenuously objects. He has the boldness or foolhardiness to " rebuke " our Lord. In impetuous, startled speech he blurts out, " This be far from Thee." His strenuous objection raises the whole question of a kingdom without sacrifice, of victory without suffering. It made the road harder to travel. The awful sharpness of the experiences which the Master plainly sees before Him is made to stand out with more painful clearness. It is hard to have one of the inner circle of His chosen band, dear, impulsive Peter, try to block the way that is clearly the Father's way for Him. And the Master plainly felt all of this.

The sharpness of His reply, the blunt plainness of His " get thee behind me, Satan," reveals at once how real was the struggle of soul, as He unhesitatingly presses on in the way marked out for Him. Here is it plain that the tempter was coming behind the warm heart, and impulsive judgment of Peter, who was quite unconscious of how he was being used. The tempter would make the way just as hard as

[1] Matthew xvi. 21-27.

he could.   The very boldness of these disguises is nothing short of startling.

The last of these illustrations is perhaps the
most subtle and telling of the four.   It came
within the last week.   It is the story of the
Greeks' request.[1]   Whether they were actual
Greeks, or from a Greek-speaking people of
some other nationality, or merely representa-
tives of a non-Jewish people, matters not.   They
were the outside non-Jewish world coming
eagerly and earnestly to our Lord.   The Jewish
door was in its last stage of shutting against
Him.   Here was the door into the whole outer
world opening.   And our Lord had come for a
world.   He had not come to Palestine merely.
That was only the doorway in.   These earnest
truth-seekers opened to Him the whole outer
world.   He could go to Athens and Corinth.
And how the Greek crowds would have yielded
to His sway.   But He knew well that only by
the red road of Joseph's tomb could He reach
Greeks and all the world, in the way His Father
had planned.

The language He used shows, with pathetic
intensity, how real was the struggle of soul of
this Man, now within a few days of the Cross.
Listen: " Now is my soul troubled.   And what
shall I say?   Shall I say, ' Father, save me from
this hour '?   No, I cannot say that, for for this

[1] John xii. 20-28.

cause came I unto this hour. This is what I
will say, ' Father, glorify Thy name, even though
it mean a cross for me.' " It was a sore hour.
It was a real temptation. Saying " no " to
these earnest Greek inquirers was one of the
hardest things the Master ever did. It is still
one of the hardest things for some of His followers to do. The tempter was making one of
his subtlest, strongest approaches behind these
earnest seekers, with their plea for light and
help, all unconscious as they were of how they
were being used.

These incidents show up at once how subtle
and how bold the tempter is in the disguises behind which he seeks to hide his approaches—a
tender-hearted mother, a warm-hearted friend
and follower, an enthusiastic admiring clamorous
crowd, earnest seekers after truth. How difficult such pleas are to turn aside our own hearts
and experiences tell us, in some part.

Our Lord detected the presence of the tempter
behind each. With all His tender-heartedness
for His mother, His love for dear Peter, His
heart-moving compassion for the multitudes, and
His quick response at all times to earnest seekers after light, He still saw that the Father's
path led Him quite aside from these.

The "Angel-of-Light" Disguise.

The tempter has a third way of hiding his approach to us. It is so strange and bold as to make it seem almost blasphemous even to repeat it. *He hides behind God!* That is to say, he pretends to be God's own messenger. Paul's way of saying it is that he "fashioneth himself into an angel of light." [1] The boldness and subtlety of this reveals the desperateness of the tempter. It reveals, too, the reality and desperateness of the fight that is on. It is a real fight; no mere make-believe.

The tempter will come to us under pretence of being God's messenger, or of being God Himself. That is to say, he will, for example, quote some bit of God's Word, so thinking to make us think it is God who is speaking. It is true that the quotation is quite apt to be a mis-quotation, or a partial quotation, or a bit taken quite out of its setting, and so away from its true meaning. But it is also true that these quotations of his are accepted by great numbers, who do not recognize the personality of the quoter.

Then, in addition to this is the other method of clothing his suggestions in religious phraseology. There is an intermingling of enough that is true and good with what is bad and not true, as to give the impression that all is good. The

[1] 2 Corinthians xi. 14.

impression he seeks to give is that it is God Himself who is talking to us, and so the impression that in adopting and following his suggestion we are really doing the thing God wants done. This may be called the religious temptation. It is his favourite way of approach to earnest, godly people.

It is most interesting that he used this disguise with our Lord. In the Wilderness he preached the Gospel of trust in God. He said, " Cast Thyself down. Trust God. He has said He will give His angels charge over Thee, and in their hands they shall bear thee up lest thou dash thy foot against a stone." Was ever preaching more plausible in sound! And was a bit of God's Word ever more pushed out of its meaning in application!

Yet the recognition of this guise is really not difficult. For in it the tempter is always suggesting something a little extreme. The method is really to make some extreme or unwarranted application of what the Word teaches. And this, be it keenly noted, is one of the sure touchstones by which to test his temptations, as we shall see a little later.

It may help to look at a few of his favourite temptations under this disguise. We are taught in Scripture to yield glad submission to God's will for our lives. There has been much preaching of this blessed truth of late years. And many have sought to make this the controlling purpose in their lives.

The tempter's perversion of this is that we are to yield to whatever comes to us, as being the will of God for us. Under that disguise he would lead us to accept as God's will much that he himself—the tempter—sends. The true spirit of submission is an *intelligent discerning* of what God's will for us is, and then a glad acceptance of it. The tempter's counterfeit is that we should *blindly* accept whatever comes, as being God's will because it has come. So he would get us to accept his own doings under the supposition that we are yielding to God's will.

There is a vast amount of misfortune, and disease, and mental depression that is so accepted. Whereas if there were a prayerful *discerning* of what is God's will, and what is not, much that comes would be steadily resisted, as an evil thing, in our Lord Jesus' Name, and so deliverance would come from it. The Master's word to " watch " as well as " pray," if used more faithfully and intelligently, would help greatly. We would find freedom from much that has mistakenly been accepted as from God.

Good, or God's Will.

A second perversion of this sort is in connection with Christian service. There is much

222 Quiet Talks about the Tempter

Christian service that is done merely because it is a good thing to do. The purpose to "do good" is the controlling thought. The true controlling purpose in service should not be to do good simply, but to do God's will. Doing God's will is always good. But doing something that is good may not be doing the thing that God has planned for us to do. There is a Lord to the harvest. We are not to start in doing the thing that strikes us as being a good thing to do. We are to find out the plan of the Lord, and fit into that. A vast amount of hit-or-miss work, and a vast amount of strength, would be turned to much better account if this "do good" fallacy were exploded.

Speaking broadly it would undoubtedly have been doing good for our Lord to have met those Greeks, and gone with them to their people to teach about the true God, and to heal their sick, and so on. But we know so well that that was not God's will for Him.

Mr. Spurgeon at one time was urged to accept an invitation to preach at a certain place. And in pressing the invitation it was stated that he would have the opportunity of speaking to a very large audience of many thousands, including very influential people. His quiet reply, as he declined going, was that he was not ambitious to preach to thousands, but only to do the will of God.

God guides the prayerful man to discern what His will of service for him is. But this thing of merely doing good rather than discerning the good that is also God's plan for us, has ever been one of the tempter's favourite temptations with religious folk. We should frequently recall the lines that run:—

> "More anxious not to serve Thee much;
> But please Thee perfectly."

A third "Angel-of-light" disguise is regarding that very sensitive stuff called money. The Jews were required to pay a tenth of all into God's treasury. And the giving of a tenth has been widely advocated as the standard of giving for *Christians*. It is a standard of giving that has been followed by many, and has brought great blessing to the givers, and loosened out much money for God's work. If the whole Church membership could be brought up to this standard the Lord's work would be revolutionized in the funds that would be loosened out for use, and immense blessing would follow to the Church itself.

That is all true. But there is more yet to be said that is true also, and that more gives an utter change of view. The giving of a tenth has been taken to mean that we are fully discharging the love obligation laid upon us by giving *only a tenth*. The Jew practically was *taxed* a tenth; the giving was not voluntary; it was compulsory. The Christian is not under any such law of compulsion. He is left free to do as his heart moves him, with very strong motives brought to play upon his heart action. The Jew had much less of light, and privilege, and fulness of blessing than the Christian.

The Jesus-passion in Control.

The tenth is an Old Testament standard. But we are living in the New Testament floodlight. The New Testament standard, in effect, is this: that everything we have is to be *controlled* by the one purpose of telling all the world of our Lord Jesus. That is the passion of our Lord's heart, and is to be the passion of ours, too, as we follow Him. Under this light we are to retain what our needs call for, that being left wholly to our individual judgment, guided by the Holy Spirit, to decide, and all the rest is to be controlled in its use by this passion of our Lord's heart.

There are thousands of Christians who conscientiously give the tenth, and some even a larger fraction than this, and then keep all the rest for themselves. Many of them live saintly lives, are devoted in their Christian service, but live in luxury, and keep the greater part of the year's income for themselves. Yet the millions are without a saving knowledge of the Saviour. And the one passionate desire of our Lord's heart remains unsatisfied, and His return is being delayed. These people follow this course conscientiously. So they have been taught to do. They are on a higher plane of giving than the majority of Christians. They have not gone past their leaders to the Word itself for its simple fuller teaching.

The common teaching about giving a tenth has loosened out vast sums, and, it has been so understood and applied, that it has held back far vaster sums that the Lord meant should be used in making Him known, and in bringing Him back. Giving a tenth has practically been taken to mean giving *only* a tenth, and that is utterly opposed to the whole New Testament teaching and spirit.

It seems quite a bit startling to say so, but without doubt the tempter's purpose to keep the millions in darkness has been furthered by the teaching that in giving a tenth we are fully doing what our Lord expects of us. It has been one of his subtlest modern disguises in withholding the Gospel of Christ from the vast majority of the human race.

These suggestions give a little inkling into the meaning hidden within that phrase, " An angel of light." The tempter has great power

of cunning in using religious phraseology. He
has fine skill in making use of much of the
commonly accepted Christian teaching in furthering his own plans.

The "How" of Training.

And now we want to talk together about how
these disguises may be quickly and surely detected.   And it is a great comfort to know
that even though the disguise be ever so cunningly made up, it can yet be easily detected. It
does not require intellectual wisdom or keenness to pierce through the most subtle disguises.
The detection comes easily to a heart kept in
tune with our Lord's heart.   It comes through
a simple training of the spirit and judgment
by the Word and by the Holy Spirit.

There are two "hows" in the answer.   One
has to do with ourselves, and the other has to
do with the tempter.   The first is in the training of our ears and eyes and touch.   The second
is in getting familiar with some of the tempter's
foot-prints.

First, the bit about our training.   The one
need here is to have keen ears, and keen eyes,
and a sensitiveness to the evil one's presence
and touch.   With these it is very important to
cultivate a simple common sense, a good poise
of judgment.   We don't want to move from

Faith Street, on the top of the hill, down into Queer Street on the slope.

The great thing here is ears trained to distinguish between the Master's voice and the tempter's. Our Lord said, " My sheep hear my voice." [1] That word " hear " means recognize. The sheep were trained, by constant contact with the shepherd, to recognize his voice, and to know at once the voice of the pretending thief. We are to be trained to recognize our Master's voice, and to know quickly that other voice that tries to deceive us by imitating His. How shall we get this faculty of quick and sure recognition?

There are three simple essentials here. They can be put very simply, and briefly, because they have been spoken of before in these Talks. The first is the act of surrender to the mastery of the Master. That is made a practical thing by the *habit* of yielding the life to Him, as each day brings new light. Surrendering is turning every last ragged remnant of the evil one, however disguised, out of doors. So only can there come clear keen eyes and ears for his approach. Any unsurrendered bit confuses both eyes and ears. It blurs the moral sense.

The second essential is in the daily quiet time, alone with the Master, over His Word. It must be daily. It must be with the Word itself. It must be quiet, unhurried, unflurried

[1] John x. 27.

time. It must be with the door shut, the outer things shut out, and one's self shut in with the Master. So the mind becomes informed. So the judgment is enlightened and moulded. So the whole being becomes saturated with God's truth. Through all of this there comes the sensible poised judgment.

The purpose here is not the Book itself, though it has the central place. It is not even for prayer, though that will have an absorbing place. It is that through the Book, and by means of the prayer, we shall come into direct touch with the Lord Jesus Himself. So the Book shall be enlightened to us. So prayer shall be a real talking with Himself. The Book itself trains the judgment. The direct touch with the Master trains the spirit.

The third essential is habitual obedience to the Spirit's voice as He speaks to your innermost heart through His Word. Obedience has a most direct influence on ears and eyes and spirit. If you obey, your spirit senses become keener, and more accurate. If you disobey, or fail to obey, in something about which you are clear, at once ears and eyes and spirit begin to get confused. Failure to obey dulls and deafens the ears. Listening to what we know is true, but what we won't obey, is ruinous to the hearing.[1]

[1] Isaiah vi. 9-13.

Mark most keenly that the whole purpose here is to get trained spirit senses, so as to recognize surely God's voice, and to detect just as surely the imitation voice that comes. These three things act directly upon the spirit senses.

The "How" of Detection.

Then there's a second "how" of detection. There are certain *Satanic ear-marks* by which his presence can be detected. And with those I want to group certain contrasted marks of God's presence. First is this: the tempter always suggests doubt of God's love. The suggestion may come direct. Or, it may come so subtly that at first you don't think of it in that way. But as you notice keenly you find the practical effect is to make you hold back because of an element of doubt about God. In contrast with this, God's touch always brings a quiet, confiding sense of trust in Himself.

A second sure ear-mark is that his suggestion is always essentially selfish. It may not seem so on the surface. But if, when sifted down, it proves to be so, it may safely be put to the tempter's account. He is very subtle here. The suggestion to our Lord behind Peter's objection, behind the Greeks' request, and behind the bread-filled multitudes, was the same—namely, that so He could be saved from the suffering otherwise involved. In contrast with this, God's touch always gives a passion for Himself. And that passion pushes self clear out, so far as it may hinder God's plan.

A third ear-mark: the tempter is apt to be in a hurry. He may at times worry you by a slow, dragging process when that suits his purposes. But he is more likely to try to rush you off your feet with a sudden quick movement. He showed our Lord all the kingdoms of the world "in a moment of time." [1] That may be conceded to be pretty swift work. He is fond of sudden moves and of rushing tactics. The serpent's voice in Eden kept egging Eve on to action. In contrast with this, note that God never moves in a hurry. He may move swiftly, but never hurriedly nor hastily. There's a quiet steady on-moving when He is guiding.

Close up to that comes this fourth ear-mark: the tempter's suggestions are apt to make one feverish. This is a sure test for ambitious plans. Any trace or taint of fever produced is a pretty sure indication of the tempter's presence. In sharp contrast with this, God's touch always makes us quiet and clear and deliberate. Our Master's touch still has the same power and effect as when He touched the hand of Peter's wife's mother; the fever leaves.

A fifth ear-mark: the tempter is fond of flat-

[1] Luke iv. 5.

tering you. There was the touch of flattery in
the Wilderness suggestion that our Lord make
bread out of the stones. He *could* make bread
out of stones, had He been so led. Such a re-
minder of one's power has the touch of flattery
in it. This is a sure ear-mark. It never fails
to tell his presence. In contrast with this, note
that the Holy Spirit never flatters. He may lead
us to recognize properly what strength we have,
or what gifts we have been entrusted with. But
with that is always the reminding sense that
these are from God, and are to be used as a
trust, and farther that they are not used up to
their best possible limit save as they are played
upon, and permeated by His Spirit.

Then the tempter has rare power of produc-
ing a sense of fear. He makes us afraid. We
hold back because of a sense of dread. Much
has already been said of this. The fear that is
afraid is a sure index finger pointing to the
unseen tempter or one of his subs. Contrasted
with this is the fact, just as sure, that God's
touch and voice bring a sense of quiet confidence in Him. His presence recognized brings
a touch of awe, always, but never of fear. When
He speaks we are willing to undertake the impossible, to dare and to endure, with equal confidence in the outcome.

Another unfailing ear-mark of the tempter's
presence is a sense of depression, either mental

or of spirit. There may be much depression of this sort due to over-tired nerves. And then, simple food, fresh air, enough sleep and exercise, and the grip of a strong purpose, will play a big part in straightening out. But depression is one of the sure ear-marks of the tempter's attack, especially with earnest, godly people. But when God's presence has sweep there is peace and joy. These are characteristic of Him. " The fruit of the Spirit is love, joy, peace. . . ." [1]

The last ear-mark to be spoken of here is one that should be noted keenly, and emphasized much. The tempter is fond of extremes. He pushes things out of their right relations. A right thing pushed out of its right place is quite apt to become a wrong thing. He likes the pendulum swing, first this extreme, then the very opposite. Truth out of right relation becomes error. Truth is fact held in right relation with the whole circle of related truth. The great theological controversies that have split the Church of Christ up so sorely have been largely due to an undue emphasis upon some phase of truth, pushed out of its due relation to other truth. And they have usually been settled by the same sort of undue emphasis. The creeds of Christendom bear witness to this.

The precious Cross of Christ through which we are saved can be degenerated into a mere

[1] Galatians v. 22.

superstitious fetish.   The blessed teaching of
our Lord's second coming can be pushed to
the extreme of calendar making, and of white-
robed people waiting up all night on the top
of some hill.   And so the sweet truth itself is
brought into contempt.   Error is flashy and
spectacular and erratic.   Truth loves the quiet
Quaker garb and speech.   In contrast with this,
it is worthy of special emphasis that the Holy
Spirit is a spirit of sanity.   No one is so poised
and sane in his judgment and actions as the
man who is swayed by the Spirit of God.

These are some of the ear-marks by which
the tempter's suggestion may be tested.   Yet,
remember, we are not to be going about eyeing
suspiciously everybody we meet.   Let us quietly,
steadily go on the way the Master points out
for us, with our face ever turned toward His,
our hearts ever in tune with His own, and our
hands stretched out in glad, warm service among
the needy.   And the Master will guide us safely
past snares as we keep close to Him, and push
on in His way.

AUTHORITY TO TAKE POSSESSION OF WHAT HAS BEEN REDEEMED FROM THE ENEMY

A New Spelling.

The defeat of the enemy gives a new power to prayer. The victory of our Lord Jesus gives a new meaning to prayer. That newness of power and meaning can best be told by a new spelling of the word " ask." " Ask " is one of the great Scripture keywords for prayer.

Six times over on that night in which He was so basely betrayed, our Lord used that word " ask " in talking with the inner circle. " Whatsoever ye shall *ask* in My name, that will I do." " If ye shall *ask* anything in My name, that will I do." " If ye abide in Me, and My words abide in you, *ask.*" " Ye did not choose Me, but I chose you, and appointed you, that ye should go and bear fruit, and that your fruit should abide; that whatsoever ye shall *ask.*" " If ye shall *ask* anything." " Ye shall *ask* in My name." [1]

Now, there is a new spelling of that little

[1] John xiv. 13, 14; xv. 7, 16; xvi. 23, 26.

word. It is given to us by our Lord Jesus. It is not spoken by His lips, but spelled out for us by what He did in defeating the tempter. It is of immense importance to us that we get this new spelling clearly in our minds and hearts. For if we do it will mean new praying, and greater results in our praying.

The new spelling is t-a-k-e. That is the Master's spelling. It is the spelling of His life, and of His Calvary death, and of that great Third Morning after. That new spelling puts the whole matter of prayer in a new light, the bright light of our Lord's victory. The old spelling is a-s-k. The difference between the two is sharply marked. We usually think of "ask" in connection with a favour which we desire. It may be granted. We hope it will be. But with it, whether rightly or wrongly, goes the impression of pleading, and persistent repetition. Coupled with that is earnest desire and longing, and also an element of uncertainty, which we attempt, more or less, to get rid of.

The word "take" suggests at once that the thing in question belongs to you by *right,* rather than as a favour you are desiring. It supposes that we have a real right to this thing we are wanting to get possession of. It is ours in fact, though not ours in actual possession; so we reach out a hand to grasp it, and so to know by the feel that we have it. "Take" suggests a check presented at the teller's counter of a bank where you have deposited funds. The check becomes a demand. You call for what is your own.

If it be true that we may properly get something of this sort into our praying it will surely make a great difference in our prayers, and in the spirit of confidence with which we will pray. May we indeed use this word " take " where we have been using " ask " ?

Five Facts.

Well, there are five simple facts which, I think, will make it quite clear that we may, and if we may surely we should, and surely we will. The first link in the chain is this: when God made man in His own image He gave him mastery over the earth.[1] He was made God's under-master over all the creation, and over all the forces of nature. Man was created a prince. He was born to rule. That was God's wondrous love-plan for man.

The second bit to note is that man lost that mastery through disobedience. It is a primary law in God's world that what He gives is held only through obedience. Disobedience demits the title. Possession is kept only through full obedience to the trust-deed. That is an abso-

[1] Genesis i. 26-28; Psalm viii. 4-8

lute law of holding what has been given to us
by God. Obedience keepeth the title intact; disobedience breaks it at once. Man was subtly
tempted to disobey. This was the tempter's
whole thought. Man yielded. He disobeyed.
In that he lost title to the dominion with which
he had been endowed. Instead of being a master over the earth, he has been, in the main, a
slave upon the earth.

The third link is this: man transferred that
mastery or dominion to the one to whom he
yielded obedience. He obeyed the evil one. In
that obedience he became his vassal, his slave.
" His servants ye are whom ye obey." [1] Our
Lord speaks of the tempter as the " prince of
this world." But we do well to remember just
what that means. He is the prince, but not the
rightful prince. He himself has been untrue to
God, and so lost his title to what was given him.
He is a traitor-prince. He deceived man into
that initial act of obedience to himself, and disobedience to God. So he became a usurper-
prince. But the word " prince " stands out in
both combinations. Though he is a traitor-
prince, and a usurper-prince, he is still prince
of this world. Man's obedience to him gave him
an actual hold, and a strong hold too, upon this
earth, and all of its life.

The fourth fact lets in a bit of glad, golden

[1] Romans vi. 16.

light. The Lord Jesus came. He was given
the mastery of the earth, and of all things, down
here, all afresh, by the Father, even as Adam
had been. He Himself said "all things have
been delivered unto me of My Father." [1] That
truth is repeated over three times in John's
Gospel. [2] He was the new Master of all
things down here. But He could hold His
mastery only by obedience. He was not an
exception to this law of title-holding. He
could not be. Obedience is an inherent law
of life.

The great fact about our Lord that stands
out in brightest light is that He was obedient.
This was the touchstone of all His life. He
obeyed, [3] even unto death, aye, the worst sort
of death, that of the Cross. Without question
the one thing the tempter aimed at all those
thirty-odd years was to make obedience by Jesus
just as hard as possible, in the hope of diverting
Him from that narrow path. But our Lord remained true. He held the title to all things by
His perfect obedience.

Then when He went back home again that
title was confirmed to Him. He was seated
"far above all rule, and authority, and power,
and every name that is named not only in this

[1] Matthew xi. 27.

[2] John iii. 35; xiii. 3; xvii. 2.

[3] Philippians ii. 8; Hebrews v. 8; Romans v. 19.

world, but also in that which is to come." [1] Mastery over all things pertaining to the earth was *given* Him by the Father. It was *held* by Him through perfect obedience. It was *confirmed* to Him on His return home. That's the fourth great link in this " take " chain.

And the fifth is this: He did all of this *on our account*. It was because we failed that He came. He did what we failed in. In all that He did He was acting in our stead. We love to talk of our Lord Jesus as our Substitute. When He climbed the Hill of the Cross, and poured out His life unto death, He was acting in our place. He was our Substitute, bearing the full brunt of our sin. Through Him, and His precious blood, we are set free. But I think, we do not use that word " Substitute " as much as we should.

Authorized.

He was a three-fold Substitute. First, in His life, by His perfect obedience in Nazareth, and on to the end of His life. He was our Substitute there. We failed in obedience. He obeyed perfectly in our place. Then on the Cross He was our Substitute, bearing the shame and death that belonged to us. And then on the Resurrec-

[1] Ephesians i. 20-22; Philippians ii. 8-11; Colossians ii. 10; 1 Peter iii. 22.

tion morning, He was still acting for us when He arose. In all of this He was acting on our behalf.

I used to wonder in my ignorance why our Lord did not finish up at once the whole conflict with the evil one. Why should Satan have been left free for these two thousand years? Why was he not put finally out of the way when once he had been so disastrously defeated? Well, the answer, after all, is a very simple one, and goes at once to the core of what we are talking about. If our Lord had been acting on His own account simply, and only, the conflict *would* have been closed up at once, and the defeated never able to do more.

But our Lord was not acting for Himself. He was acting for us. And there is something for us to do in settling the conflict. We must accept as our own what was done for us. *We must step in and take possession of what had been our own originally, and what is now won back for us.* Our Master practically says, "Take possession of what I have redeemed, what I have bought back for you."

Do you remember that marvellous statement of His in the tenth chapter of Luke?[1] That is a passage that ought to be marked in our Bibles in red, or in gold, or any way that will make it stand out big and plain to our eyes.

[1] Luke x. 18-19.

Listen to it prayerfully, that its tremendous meaning may come home to our innermost hearts. *"Behold, I have given you authority* to tread upon serpents and scorpions, and *over all the power of the enemy;* and nothing shall in any wise hurt you."* And in the midst of the glad rejoicing that such words must bring He adds that our chief rejoicing is to be over what He has done for us. It is all of His wondrous grace that we have such wondrous power.

Now, we should *use* this authority given to us; use it in Jesus' great Name; use it as the Holy Spirit guides; use it as the need comes in our lives, and in the opposition that is aroused by service. We have authority to take from the enemy everything he is holding back. The chief way of taking is by prayer, and by whatever action prayer leads us to. The cry that should be ringing out to-day is this great cry of "Take, in Jesus' great Name."

In my Master's Name I would speak out this message of His all anew to every follower of His in any need or stress. To these out on the far-flung, thin, red firing line of the foreign mission-field, in the midst of Africa's savagery, of China's opposition and apathy, of India's crying need, to those in the midst of London's slums and streets, in the thick and drive of New York's push and scramble; to any one and every one, wherever the stress of sin and of need is

being felt. This is His message to you to-day.
Listen keenly, " I, Jesus, have given you authority over all the power of the enemy. I *have*
the authority. I have won it by my own life-
blood. I won it for you. I give it to you. Use
it in my name. Greater works shall ye do because I am with the Father in the place of
authority, and you shall act in my place even as
I acted in your place."

Take Possession.

This is the word that needs sounding out most
clearly everywhere to-day. Use the authority
the Master has given you. Take whatever is
needed in His holy service. " Every place that
the sole of your foot shall tread upon, to you
have I given it." [1] *Take* what the Master has
brought back for us. Asking means taking. It
doesn't mean pleading with God as though to
persuade Him. He is more eager than we. It
means claiming as our very own whatever is
needed. It means taking possession by faith of
what our great Captain has won back for us.

The last message of our Lord's lips, on Olivet,
fits in here with peculiar power. Listen: " All
authority hath been given unto Me in heaven
and on earth. Go ye *therefore*." [2] That little

[1] Joshua i. 3.
[2] Matthew xxviii. 18, 19.

preposition " on " in " on the earth " could accurately be made to read " over." He has been given all authority on the earth and over the earth. It is because of that authority that we are bidden to " go." We go because of His authority. We go authorized as His plenipotentiaries. That " go " underlies all Christian service. As we " go " we will need not only power but authority, for every step of our ongoing is contested. In that authority we are to go, and to take what is our rightful possession, in the Name of our Substitute-Victor.

As your service leads you on to a bit of ground that is held by the forces of evil remember this; that bit of ground belongs to man, to be held by him for God. It has been lost through disobedience. But it has been won back by the Victor. You have the right to step in and say, " I take, in the name of the Lord Jesus, I take this bit of the earth back for Him; I take the life of *this* man, and *this* man, for whom my Master gave His blood."

But—*but* the taking must be as deep as your life; it must be as intense as the opposition. Satan is a stiff fighter; he doesn't yield except *what* he must. The taking must be definite. Prayer must always be *definite*. He does not yield until he must. He is a stubborn fighter. Prayer must be *persistent*. The taking must be as insistent as the enemy is persistent, and just a bit more; and there's where the fight comes. The man whom you are trying to win for God, maybe in London, maybe your loved one, maybe in North Africa or South Africa, wherever he is—that man whom you would have come to Jesus Christ, he *belongs* to Him through His victory. You take him, in Jesus Christ the Victor's name, and insist on taking, and the rest will always come. The new spelling, the Calvary spelling of "*ask*" is T-A-K-E, take, in Jesus Christ the Victor's name.

This brings to us all anew with fresh force the old fact that our Lord gave us the right to use His name. He could have done no greater thing. Using His Name is, in effect, acting as Himself, clothed with all of His power. But it is a serious thing to use that Name. Every one may not use it. Only those who have accepted His invitation into the inner circle with Himself may use it. You remember the men in that Ephesus story in the nineteenth chapter of Acts. They tried to use that name for their own selfish purposes. And the evil spirits leaped upon them and left them wounded and bleeding. The demon world knows full well about that Name, and its great power. It is feared there. And they know, too, who may use it.

If you will turn to that last long talk[1] in which the Master gave us the right to use His name, you will find certain words occurring repeatedly. The words "love" and "obey" and "abide" underlie the right to use the Name. Love obeys. It loves to obey. Love abides. The other way of spelling abide is o-b-e-y. The other way of spelling love is o-b-e-y. Obedience is the clear title to the right to use that Name—the obedience of love. Obey as fully and gladly as an obedient child obeys. Hold the whole life open to the Master's touch and control. Then you may ask what you will. You may take what you choose. And the usurper will loosen his hold, slowly, angrily, but surely, and you shall have in actual possession what you have "taken" by faith.

Faith that Discerns.

And that word "faith" ought to have another word, too. It will help us to remember just what faith is, in practical effect. Faith is knowing that our Lord Jesus *is* Victor. That is to say, it is not thinking about how much faith you have. It is thinking about Him. And it is not thinking so much about what He *will* do. It is thinking most about what He *has* done. Jesus Christ is Victor. Faith is depending on

[1] John xiv.-xvi.

that, or, better yet, on *Him*. It is not working up your feelings, and saying, " I must believe "; not that. It is simply fixing my whole thought on Jesus, the Victor. There He is on the throne. That scarred, crowned, enthroned Lord Jesus— I have no doubt about Him. That is faith— looking to Him, resting on what He is, and what he has done.

There's still another simple word to put in here that we may keep things in poise. A " taking " faith is a *discerning* faith. Those words " obey " and " abide " point to the close touch with the Master that lets us know what His plans are. The daily study of His Word reveals to us His will, and trains us to discern what His particular will is under the circumstance where you must act. Abiding makes us keen to know what we may take. The whole purpose underneath everything is to get His great loving will done. There must be a clear eye before there can be a taking hand.

As I step quietly on, under the gracious guidance of His Spirit, I am to " take " what I will, in His Name—life after life, man after man, gold after gold, strength renewed constantly for new work, anything and everything that is needed, and that should be in His service. And because He is Victor, every hindrance must go, and will go, before the man who presses forward where He leads in His Name.

Power in the Name.

Recently I was up in Sweden. Sitting across the table from me was a missionary from North Africa, from Tunis. One day she told us this story. She had a friend, a sister missionary in Algiers. And this sister missionary told her of an Arab woman whom she had won to Christ. The Arab woman was a Mohammedan, with all the fanaticism, ignorance and superstition that marks that strange Mohammedan belief or superstition. This woman was won for Christ. Her family did their best to sway her from her new faith. They coaxed, pleaded, argued, threatened, made her life miserable, but she showed the quality of her faith by her firm, quiet stand. She could not be moved. She knew she was right.

Then they did what is characteristic of that people, they concocted a poison, very subtle, very deadly, and put it into her food, of course secretly. When she had eaten the meal in which the poison had been introduced, she knew quickly what had taken place. She felt the poison. She knew full well about the poison, how deadly it was. She knew the habit of her people. As she felt the thing in her blood, she knew instantly what had happened. And she knew this, that through the poison she was doomed to death. She knew it. You can fancy just how she felt as the poison worked. It would make one very irritable and mean in spirit, then very dull in mind, then it would affect the mind still more, and then the body, until death would come. That was the course it usually ran. And she was greatly startled and greatly distressed, and didn't know what to do.

As she sat at the table, I think without planning it, she commenced to repeat the Name, the great Name. She could not repeat it aloud, for that would mean persecution by those around her. And so to herself, with all the intensity of one who felt the sentence of death in her body, she commenced to repeat that marvellous Name above every name, "Jesus! *Jesus!!* JESUS!!!" For two days or three, my friend was not sure which, that went on, and the poison gradually receded from the woman's body, from her blood, while the family watched her with strange eyes. This was something new. The poison had never failed before. But it was failing.

And as she herself told the story to the missionary, she said, "I felt as though each time I said that Name it was like a wave of life coming in; and in between like a wave of death." And the conflict between life and death went on for those days, but the death becoming less and the life more, until at the end of the second day or the third, she was free, to their utter astonishment, and to her own great joy.

That was a victory in the body, a possible thing as the Holy Spirit guides. But it is only a bit of the larger possibility. We have the right, as we are obedient, to use that Name. As we do use it, under the Holy Spirit's guidance, going step by step as He leads, we may take out of the hand of the evil one, men, and women, and property, and gold, and all that we need, because the Lord Jesus has said—" All authority hath been given unto me over all the earth." Shall we go out and take, in Jesus' Name, what belongs to us by the right of His death and resurrection?

By G. CAMPBELL MORGAN

Expository

The Study and Teaching of the English Bible.
Cloth, - - - - - net $.50

The Missionary Manifesto. Being a Study of the Great
Commission - - - - net .75

The Analyzed Bible. 8vo, Cloth. each, - net 1.00
Vols I, II, III, Introductory Volumes. Vol. IV, The Gospel According to John. Vol. V, The Book of Job. Vol. VI, Romans Vols. VII, VIII, The Prophecy of Isaiah, I and II. *Other Volumes to follow.*

The Parables of the Kingdom. Expositions of Matt. XIII.
- - - - - - net 1.00

The Crises of the Christ. *Popular Edition,* net 1.50

The Spirit of God. Cloth, - - - net 1.25

A First Century Message to Twentieth Century Christians. - - - - net 1.00

God's Methods With Man. In Time—Past, Present and
Future. With Colored Chart, - - 1.00

Wherein Have We Robbed God? - - .75

God's Perfect Will. - - - net .50

The Ten Commandments. - - - net .50

The Hidden Years at Nazareth. - - net .25

Devotional

Christian Principles, 16mo, Cloth, - - net .50

Mountains and Valleys in the Ministry of Jesus. 18mo,
Boards, - - - - net .25

The Practice of Prayer. 12mo, Cloth, - net .75

The Simple Things of the Christian Life. 16mo, Cloth,
- - - - - net .50

The True Estimate of Life and How to Live. An entirely
new. enlarged and revised edition. Gilt Top, net .80

The Christ of To-day. What? Whence? Whither?
- - - - - net .35

The Life of the Christian. - - - net .50

Evangelism. - - - - net .50

Life Problems. - - . - . .50

Discipleship. - - - - .50

"All Things New." A Message to New Converts. Paper,
- - - - - net .10

Christ and the Bible. 16mo, Paper, - net .05

119